God Is One

The Way of Islam

R. Marston Speight

Friendship Press • New York

Notes:

1. All translations from the Arabic Qur'an are by the author.
2. Much material in this book has been adapted from the author's book, *Christian-Muslim Relations: An Introduction for Christians*, 3rd edition. Hartford: The Office on Christian-Muslim Relations of the National Council of the Churches of Christ in the USA, 1986.
3. In conformity to Islamic practice, the masculine pronoun has been used when referring to God.

The illustrative material boxed on various pages of this book was prepared by editor Carol M. Ames and researcher Kristine M. Rogers, Ph.D., with counsel and contributions from the author, R. Marston Speight. A complete list of citations for all copyrighted material and other acknowledgements are found on pages 138-139.

Library of Congress Cataloging-in-Publication Data
Speight, R. Marston, 1924-
    God is one.
    1. Islam. 2. Christianity and other religions—Islam. 3. Islam—Relations—Christianity. I. Title.
BP161.2.S64 1989   297   88-33424
ISBN 0-377-00196-1

ISBN 0-377-00196-1
Editorial Offices: 475 Riverside Drive, Room 772, New York, NY 10115
Distribution Offices: P.O. Box 37844, Cincinnati, OH 45222-0844
Copyright © 1989 Friendship Press, Inc.
Printed in the United States of America

Contents

1

Why Is It Important To Know About Islam?

*M*any centuries ago, when a few people of Arabia started to follow the Prophet Muhammad, they encountered serious opposition from their neighbors in the city of Mecca. Most Meccans considered Muhammad to be a religious fanatic who was making preposterous claims about being a prophet of the one and only God of the universe. Finally, after he saw that his friends and followers were being harassed beyond measure, Muhammad advised a group of them, about a hundred, to take temporary refuge in the neighboring country of Ethiopia, because, he said, the king of Ethiopia is a Christian. He will protect you until such time as it is advisable for you to return to Mecca.

When the refugees reached Ethiopia, they were taken before the Christian king of that land, called the Najashi. In the royal presence a question was put to them: "What do you say about Jesus?" The spokesman for the group replied, "We say about Jesus that which our Prophet has told us (may blessings and peace be upon him): Jesus is the servant and messenger of God, the spirit and word of God whom God entrusted to the Virgin Mary." When the Najashi heard that testimony, he took a stick from the ground and said, "I swear, the difference between what we believe about Jesus, Son of Mary, and what you have said does not exceed the width of this stick."

This simple, though incomplete, discovery of what Christians had in common with the followers of Muhammad strikes the keynote of this book. As spiritual descendants of the Najashi, we Christians are taking part today in an unprecedented encounter with spiritual descendants of that little band of Arabian refugees. In this study we will be examining some of the terms and conditions of this meeting.

As we consider the question that is the title of this chapter, "Why is it important to know about Islam?" it will be helpful to have some essential preliminary information about the religion that is followed by millions of people throughout the world.

Some Basic Words

The word "Islam" comes from the Arabic language and means "submission to God," or "total commitment to the authority and power of God." Since for centuries "Islam" has also been the name of a religion, we can define it as the community or the way of life of people who unite in their submission to God according to the teachings of that particular religion. To pronounce Islam correctly, make the "i" short, the "s" as in "sit," say the "a" as in "cat" or in "father" (it is said differently in different parts of the world), and accent the last syllable, "-lam".

"Muslim" is another word we shall encounter often in this book. A Muslim is a person who belongs to the religion of Islam. This word, also from Arabic, means "one who is submitted to God, wholly committed to the divine power and authority." Speakers of Arabic use the feminine form, *Muslima*, as well as the masculine *Muslim*. However, only the masculine form has crossed into the English language. To pronounce it correctly, say the "u" as in "put," the "s" as in "sit," and accent the first syllable, "Mus-." The spelling "Moslem," although still widely used, is not recommended, simply because it leads to a pronunciation of the word that Muslims do not regard as authentic.

Muslims Are Our Neighbors

When we speak of Muslims as our neighbors, we use "neighbors" in two ways: the literal sense of close proximity, that is, people who live near us; and the extended sense of people across the earth who are linked with us by airlines, radio, television and the press, so that the world has become truly a community of neighbors.

The peoples of Islam make up one of the most numerous groups of our neighbors in both senses. Nearly one of every five human beings is a Muslim—about a billion people.

It is important to know about Islam because of the sheer number of its adherents.

There is almost no country on earth without some groups of Muslims, and in such countries as Pakistan, Saudi Arabia or Turkey, the populations are almost wholly Muslim. Later on in this book we shall learn about some of the rich cultural variety

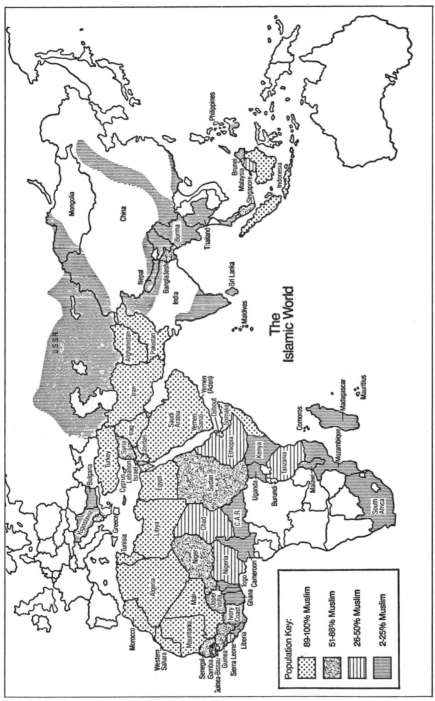

The Islamic World

Population Key:

89-100% Muslim

51-88% Muslim

26-50% Muslim

2-25% Muslim

that exists in different parts of the Islamic world.

Some people are surprised to learn that Muslims are our near neighbors in the United States and Canada. In fact, Islam is perhaps the fastest growing religion on the North American continent, today numbering nearly three million adherents, most of whom are Canadian and American citizens, not aliens. Of course, Muslims are still a small percentage of the total population of the U.S. and Canada, and it is as a minority that they live in many other areas of the world. But even as a religious minority, Muslims are an articulate and vital element in the national life of many countries. Later we shall say more about North American Muslims as well as about the Islamic populations of Western Europe.

In a rapid glance at the scope of Islam, we look first at the largest countries that have high percentages of Islamic believers, and then at the solidly Islamic states, those with overwhelming majorities of people that belong to this faith.

In the category of nations whose Muslims number up to 25 percent of the population, several are in Africa: among these are Cameroon, Ghana, Ivory Coast, Liberia and Mozambique. Two, Bulgaria and Yugoslavia, are in Eastern Europe. Three other countries with sizable percentages of Muslims may surprise some readers. Israel, which we usually think of as a solidly Jewish state, has a Muslim population that is a vital part of its economic, social and cultural life. India, where Muslims make up 12 percent of the total, and the USSR, with 18 percent, are extraordinary cases, in that their Muslim minorities, 90 million and 50 million respectively, number far more than do the whole populations of most countries with Muslim majorities.

A second category includes countries whose Muslims constitute from a quarter to a half of the total population. These nations are all in Africa; the largest are Ethiopia, Nigeria, Sierra Leone and Tanzania.

Next are nations where from 50 percent to 88 percent of the people are Muslims. Notable among these are Albania in Eastern Europe; the African countries of Sudan, Chad, Guinea, Mali and Niger; the Middle Eastern nations of Syria and Lebanon; and in South Asia, Malaysia and the archipelago nation of Indonesia. Indonesia has a larger number of Muslims than any other nation: about 145 million.

Finally, nations whose populations are remarkably homogeneous in that 89 to 100 percent are Muslim form a long list. The largest of these nations are: Afghanistan, Algeria, Bangladesh,

Egypt, Iran, Iraq, Jordan, Libya, Morocco, Pakistan, Saudi Arabia, Senegal, Somalia, Tunisia, Turkey and Yemen, both North and South.

To close this statistical survey of the Muslim world, we note the six countries that have the most Muslims, regardless of what percentage of the total population they may represent. These giants are: Indonesia, with 145 million; Pakistan, with 92 million; Bangladesh, with 90 million; India, also with 90 million; the USSR, with 50 million; and Turkey, with 50 million. It should be noted that none of these largest Islamic populations is Arab, contrary to the common misconception that most Muslims are Arabs. Although Islam began in the land of the Arabs, its non-Arab adherents vastly outnumber the Arab Muslims.

Our Debt to the Civilizing Course of Islam

Without the early philosophers, scientists, architects and artists of Islam, the brilliant achievements of twentieth-century science and technology would not have been possible. During a long period of intellectual and social decay in Christian Europe, Islamic peoples built a rich and distinguished civilization. While

Early Centers of Learning

Medieval Islamic scientists studied astronomy at observatories; the most famous were at Maragha and Samarkand. Their skills in visual observation, mathematics and instrument design led to advances in cartography, optics and calculations of celestial movements.

Even earlier, scholars of many nations began to work at such Islamic libraries as the noted House of Wisdom at Baghdad (established in 830), translating and writing works of religion, mathematics, science, philosophy and literature.

Illustration by Michael Grimsdale, courtesy of *Aramco World*, Jan./Feb. 1986.

Some Contributions of Muslim Cultures to Western Language and Life

sherbet—from the Arabic *sharbat,* which simply means "drink" though it came early to refer in particular to a sweet watery drink.

tulips—from Persia via Turkey, then Italy and France. The original Persian word was *dulband* and meant "turban" or "turban-shape."

taffeta—from the Persian *taftah,* meaning "twisted" or "woven with a twist."

damascene—Damascus was famous for its magnificent swords and daggers, which underwent a special decorative process known as "damascening."

admiral—from the French *amiral,* which came from the Arabic *amir al-* or "commander of the...," whatever the armed force might be. The arabic term did not refer to the navy in particular, but to any armed force.

yoghurt—totally Turkish in origin of name and process of making.

Other Islamic contributions: musical instruments and notation; the crafts of carpet-weaving, ceramics and glass-making; Arabian horses, gum Arabic, Turkish tobacco, Moroccan leather, Iraqi dates, Turkish towels and Turkish baths (Middle Eastern importations with largely incidental Turkish connections); the game of chess; such common words as coffee, tariff, jar, lemon, rice, lilac, apricot (through Arabic from Greek), cotton, satin (through Arabic from a Chinese port-name), and talc.

Adapted from "What the West borrowed from the Middle East" by G. M. Wickens in *Introduction to Islamic Civilization,* edited by R. M. Savory (Cambridge: Cambridge University Press, 1987), pp. 120-125.

Europe went through its so-called "Dark Ages," Islamic peoples experienced a golden age of prosperity and achievement. Then when Europeans began to revive intellectual and scientific activity, it was the Muslims' previous efforts that enabled this Renaissance to succeed. During this reawakening, the immense cultural heritage from ancient Greece and the Far East reached Europe through Latin translations of Arabic books, themselves inspired by the philosophy and science of the ancients.

It is important to know about Islam because that religion and way of life have provided important basic elements of modern civilization.

The inventive genius and intellectual curiosity, the breadth of vision and the practicality of those early Muslims were astonishing. One way to appreciate, even if only in a fragmentary way, the contribution of the Muslims to our way of life is to notice words in our language that have been borrowed from Arabic. The Arabic language was used by scientists and authors in all parts of the ancient Muslim world.

"Zero" comes from *sifr* in Arabic and points to the fact that we owe our numbering system and its use in arithmetic to the

"Tabby" cloth was imported into medieval England from the 'Attabiyah quarter of Baghdad (first called *'attabi*, then *tabi*). Its irregularly striped pattern gave the name "tabby" to a new breed of cats that began to make its appearance in England at the end of the 17th century. Not long after that, Dr. Samuel Johnson complained that the new-fangled tabbies were driving out the true English black-and-white breed. But within a century, tabbies were acclaimed as "the true English cat." Drawing by Penny Williams-Yaqub, courtesy of *Aramco World*, May-June 1987.

Muslims, who in turn had learned its rudiments from India. Islamic scholars were especially strong in mathematics; algebra and trigonometry as we know them are based upon their development of those disciplines. The word "algebra" comes from *al-jabr*, the Arabic name for that branch of mathematics.

Many names of stars are taken directly from the Arabic, thus testifying to Muslims' pioneering research in astronomy.

"Chemistry," "alkali," "alcohol" and "antimony" are examples of Arabic loan words that reflect pre-modern Islamic studies in science. Some Islamic research in the field of optics ranks among the most important in the history of science.

The gap between modern medicine and that of the ancients is so great that it is sometimes difficult to see how dependent we are on the medical knowledge of the era we call "pre-scientific." However, the ancient Muslim physicians and surgeons were such towering influences, both in theory and in practice, that the whole of Europe relied on their teachings until the seventeenth century.

Muslims excelled in agricultural and civil engineering. They were great builders, artists and artisans. Among the crafts which they developed to a high degree and by which they influenced the progress of Western manufacturing were bookbinding, weaving and metalwork. Modern decorative art owes an incalculable debt to their skills, of which the "arabesque" is a splendid example. Many common English words related to these skills, such as "cotton," "divan," "sofa," "mattress," "damask," and "muslin," come directly from Arabic.

The Impact of Recent History

We need a keen sense of history to help us understand the centuries-long process of encounters between Muslims and Christians. Over the last quarter-century Islamic peoples have come to the forefront of the world scene—often in ways that seem filled with tumult and conflict—and many North Americans have been taken aback, confused and even angered at what seem to be unreasonable, irrational and fanatical actions by Muslims.

It is important to know about Islam because of the prominent place that the peoples of that religion occupy in current affairs.

Are Muslims naturally and inevitably enemies of the Jews? Is the conflict between Israel and her neighbors a quarrel between Jews and Muslims? Why can there be no peace in the Holy Land? Are Muslims, Jews and Christians going to dispute forever over the city of Jerusalem? Why do the Iranians hate America? Does their religion make them warlike? Why the Iran-Iraq war? What is behind the Lebanese tragedy? How can we come to terms with the oil-rich nations whose peoples are largely Muslims? What does it mean to have an Islamic government in this modern age? What is the revival of Islam of which we hear so much? Does Islam encourage terrorism? These are some of the urgent questions asked by perplexed people who keep up with the daily news. Although we cannot answer all these questions in our brief study, one of the first steps towards seeking satisfactory answers is to learn the fundamentals of Islam.

Pervasive Stereotypes

People hold many stereotypes about Islam. And Muslims are deeply offended at the ways in which their religion is misrepresented in the mass media and by the public in North America. These stereotypes are false first because they are oversimplifications. For example, it is often stated that Muslims are fanatically religious people. Some adherents of Islam are certainly fanatical, but that is no reason to think that all, or even most, of them are.

Second, the stereotypes are false because they are based on false comparisons. For example, we often hear that Islam is a burdensome and legalistic religion. Such statements come from Christians who loosely compare the legal system of Islam with the Christian repudiation of legalism. This is a faulty comparison, because the legal system of Islam is not the same as the legalism against which Christian faith takes its stand.

Gifts of Healing
Islamic medicine began in the late seventh century as Muslim scientists and physicians recovered what remained of the Greek medical tradition and added observations of their own plus learnings from the Persians, the Indians and even the Chinese. Through the later work of Muslims like the great philosopher-physician Ibn Sina (Avicenna; died 1037) this store of medical knowledge was handed on to Europeans. This leaf from a manuscript of Dioscorides gives a recipe for cough medicine and shows a doctor preparing it. The manuscript is thirteenth-century Islamic from Mesopotamia. Photo: all rights reserved, The Metropolitan Museum of Art, Rogers Fund, 1913 (13.152.6).

In the third place, the stereotypes are false because they are based on inaccurate information. One often hears the opinion that Islam is a religion whose doctrinal content is rather elementary, or shallow. Those who thus judge Muslims' faith have never pored over the vast collections of legal and theological books, the encyclopedias and dictionaries, the commentaries and poetry, the instructional manuals and guidebooks, the histories and biographies that Muslims inspired by their beliefs have produced in every century.

Stereotypes themselves are barriers to understanding, but even more serious is the attitude behind these false images. Described simply, this attitude is the tendency to believe the worst about people who are not like ourselves, and in particular, people of another religion. Unfriendly and fault-finding, this attitude deals with another religion by considering it inferior and its people outside the realm of religious truth.

It is important to know about Islam in order to help eliminate the sterotypes that hinder friendly relations between people of different faiths.

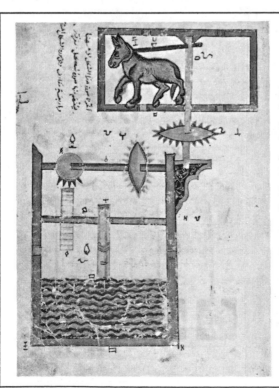

Practical Science
This design for a machine to raise water to a higher level is from *Automata*, a treatise on mechanical devices, by Abu'l Izz Isma'il al-Jazari, thought to have been a fourteenth-century Syrian scientist-engineer. Photo: all rights reserved, The Metropolitan Museum of Art, Rogers Fund, 1955 (55.212.11).

Some readers may not be aware of pervasive stereotypes about Islam. One way to test the influence of these preconceived notions is to ask ourselves: What comes to mind when we hear the words "Muhammad," "the Qur'an," "Islam"? Unfortunately, even such a brief exercise quickly surfaces negative judgments and critical opinions, because we live in an environment that is generally unfriendly to Muslims.

The Witness of the Church

Muslims make up a large part of the world in which the Christian church has felt called by God to carry out its mission across geographic frontiers. Christians seek to draw near to people of all nations in order to render service in the name of their Lord and to bear witness to the joy and power of life lived by faith in God as revealed in Jesus Christ. The "all nations" to which Christians go include multitudes of fervent believers in religions other than Christianity. Contrary to some traditional missionary thinking, these believers are *not* living in a religious void that might be filled with the message brought by Christians.

When Christians come into contact with other believers, what happens is a meeting—an encounter—between Christianity and another religion. At this time in the history of Christian missions, our encounter with Islam takes on unusual significance.

In many respects Christians feel obliged to take Islam more seriously than ever before. Muslims are telling the world that they, as well as Christians, are people who cross frontiers, that their faith is intended to be a blessing for the whole world, that they are called to spread Islam wherever it is not known. So this modern encounter between two dynamic, missionary religions produces disconcerting reactions. Christians have usually felt that it was *their* role to take the initiative and to go forth into the world, and that those to whom they went would respond (with more or less receptiveness) to their witness. But when modern Christianity meets modern Islam, we find *two* religions moving out into the whole world, both of them inspired by a vision of spreading their faith among all peoples. How do we Christians respond to this situation?

It is important to learn about Islam in order to be faithful Christian witnesses in the encounter between Christian and Muslim peoples.

Although this book is not intended to deal specifically with the principles and practice of Christian mission, it will supply some important background information for missionary thinking and suggest some ways to carry out mission, ways we feel shape a responsible and faithful response to the modern meeting of two historic and vital religious communities.

Conclusion: A Word About Approach

I have given a five-fold answer to the question, "Why is it important to know about Islam?"   And in the process I have provided a short introduction to this book's contents. Now I want to point out the ruling principle in my approach to the subject of Islam: it is founded on the Golden Rule, as expressed by Jesus in the Sermon on the Mount (Matthew 7:12).   This precept of ethical behavior states that we should do to others as we would have others do to us. In describing Islam, I shall try to present its ideals and standards, its history and development while holding as closely as I can to the way in which Muslims themselves describe it. Of course I cannot do this completely, because I am writing as an outsider, albeit a sympathetic one, to the religion. But I can abstain from picking at faults in Islam, casting it deliberately in a bad light and emphasizing the human weaknesses of some of its leaders. That is the way I would like Muslims to present the Christian faith when they have occasion to describe it. I would be disappointed if they chose to dwell on some of the petty and unworthy aspects of the church's history. I would like best for them to describe Christianity in terms of its highest and noblest ideals, the way it wants to be known in the world. So as we proceed, author and readers, let us see if we can keep to the measure of the Golden Rule.

2

The Foundation of Islam

*T*he foundation of Islam is historical, personal, scriptural and doctrinal. These aspects form a fourfold outline for describing how the religion began.

The Historical Setting

Islam arose among the Arabs who inhabited the arid, million-square-mile peninsula that today includes Saudi Arabia, the United Arab Emirates, Oman, and Yemen, North and South. The Arabs are Semitic people, which means that their language is akin to those of the Hebrews and of other peoples of the ancient Near East. At the beginning of the seventh century, their desert homeland, which looms so large on a map of the area, had been somewhat bypassed by the influential currents of world civilization. Arabia had enjoyed its glory in previous centuries, and its territory was still a channel of trade and communication between continents. Its products—spices, perfumes, hides, livestock and dates—although limited in scope, were in demand. But the centers of world power flourished elsewhere. Among these, two "superpowers" influenced the story of early Islam. To the north and west lay the Byzantine Empire, with its Greek-speaking capital at Constantinople, where Europe and Asia almost touch. To the northeast lay the Persian Empire. These giants were engaged in a constant struggle for power and, as superpowers do, both sought to gain the loyalty and support of the Arabs, by fair means or foul.

The Arabs remained apart from events of world politics in part because they were completely disunited socially and politically. Many lived as nomads, and the whole population was organized loosely into tribes, or extended family groupings. They had no centralized authority beyond that agreed upon by the family or by confederations of families. So, although individuals felt intense loyalty to their tribe, beyond that intimate tie of kinship was little or no sense of social cohesion. Strife between tribes was constant. Each group acted as a law unto itself.

In addition to the nomads, with their flocks and herds always on the move, other Arab groups practiced agriculture in fixed locations, and in a few small cities artisans and tradespeople followed a way of life much like that in other parts of the ancient world.

It was in one of the busiest and largest of these Arabian cities that the story of Islam began. Mecca was a commercial and religious center in the western sector of the Arabian Peninsula, not far from the Red Sea. The Arabs worshiped many gods, and Mecca was a place of pilgrimage, the site of one of their most revered sanctuaries. This shrine, called the *Ka'ba*, was a cube-shaped structure built around a mass of meteorite material that had been held in veneration for centuries. Looking back at this early period when the Arabs worshiped idols and spirits, Muslins call it the "time of ignorance," because in general, people had no knowledge of the one true God and no scripture to guide them.

Besides the polytheistic worshipers, there were also some Christians living in the Arabian peninsula. A few Arab tribes had turned to Christianity, which by this time was more than six hundred years old and had gone through great theological and ecclesiastical upheavals, especially in the area now known as the Middle East. The Greek Orthodox Church held the upper hand by virtue of its identification with the political power of Byzantium. But in areas adjacent to Arabia, Orthodoxy was opposed by the Monophysite Churches and the Nestorians, two branches of Christianity issuing from a dispute over the divine and human natures of Jesus Christ. One commercial center, Najran, south of Mecca, was largely inhabited by Christians.

There were Jews in Arabia, too—farmers, artisans and commercial people who had identified almost completely with Arabian life. They gave their children Arab names and adopted the social organization and customs of the area. Many of them were Arabs who had left their polytheistic faith to adopt the Jewish belief in one God.

Zoroastrianism, from Persia, was yet another religious influence in seventh-century Arabia.

Finally, the Muslim sources of information refer to individual pious believers in one God who were neither Jews, Muslims nor Christians, and who were not organized into any sect. They

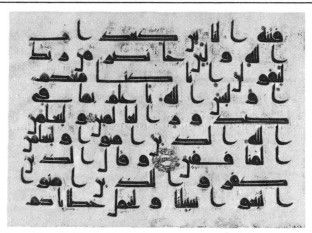

The Earliest Qur'anic Calligraphy
Portions of the Qur'an, suras 27, 28, 29. From a late ninth- or early tenth-century manuscript written in Persia in large Kufic letters, in black ink with notations in red. Kufic is the style of calligraphy most closely associated with the Qur'an and the first in which it was written in Arabic. Photo: The Pierpont Morgan Library, New York. M. 712 F. 21v.

were called *hanifs*. Muslims, who revere the Prophet Abraham as the main example from ancient times of true faith in the One God, say that in the period just before the foundation of Islam, the hanifs were the most authentic representatives of the faith of Abraham.

The birth of Islam considerably changed political and social conditions for the Arabs. Tribes united in loyalty to the new faith and organized their lives around the code of behavior that Islam prescribed. All political and economic activities were considered to be integrated and given direction by the faith. This new unity set the stage for Islam to become, over the following few centuries, a world religion. The Muslims—not the Arabs alone, but the many peoples who composed the new community of faith—were soon to become a "superpower" themselves.

The Personal Factor: Muhammad the Prophet

Islam did not just appear full-blown as a religion and way of life. It developed out of the travail and mystery of one man's story. In the view of Muslims, God revealed the new faith, little by little, to his servant, Muhammad. And that faith immersed

Muhammad in a highly dramatic series of events covering a span of twenty-three years.

Into the Meccan life of austere desert surroundings, busy commercial activities and varied religious expressions, Muhammad was born about 570 A.D. His father died just before his birth, so his grandfather, and later his uncle, raised the boy. For forty years he lived a private life, nurtured in the best tradition of a respectable, but not rich, Meccan family. We know nothing about any formal education for Muhammad. Although writing was practiced in Arabia, it was not needed then to the extent that it would be in later, more literate environments. But as we know from many examples, the complexity of languages and cultures does not depend on written literature. The principal art of the Arabs was poetry, which was transmitted orally from one generation to another. And so we can assume that Muhammad became versed in the rich oral traditions of his people.

As might be expected, given the predominant activity of Meccan society, the sources tell us that Muhammad became a commercial agent, beginning work at the age of twenty for a

---

Calligraphy—The Spirit of the Art

The Word of God came to Islam through the Qur'an. Calligraphy is thus the visual body of the divine revelation, sacred in both form and content. Corresponding to the iconographic image of Christ in Christianity, this calligraphy embodies the Word and its very presence obviates the use of any imagery. The sensible form of the Arabic language, its very sound and utterances, constitutes the most sacred art of Islam.

The very structure of calligraphy, composed of horizontal and vertical strokes woven into a fabric of profound richness, is potent with cosmological symbolism. The verticals, like the warp of a carpet, provide an ontological relationship as well as a structure for the design, while the horizontals, like the weft, correspond to the creation that develops the balance and flow of the basic conception. It is through the harmonious weaving of the horizontal and the vertical that unity is achieved....

Two main scripts have developed, from which multiple variations have evolved. *Kufic*, the earliest form, accentuates the vertical strokes of the characters and is more geometric in configuration than the cursive *nasta'liq* style.... Here strong horizontal lines, spiralling round forms, and dynamic verticals combine to create elegant manifestations of the Logos.

N. Ardalan and L. Bakhtiar, *The Sense of Unity: The Sufi Tradition in Persian Architecture.* © 1973, The University of Chicago. All rights reserved.

rich woman named Khadija. His employer was a widow, twenty years older than he, but in spite of the disparity in their ages, she was so attracted by the qualities of Muhammad's personality that she proposed marriage to him. His acceptance, at age twenty-five, led to a long and happy union that lasted another quarter-century, until Khadija died.

During the years of his private life, the future Prophet of Islam gained the respect of his community. He was called Al-Amin, or "the reliable one," by his associates and neighbors. Although he grew up in a family devoted to worship at the Ka'ba, Muhammad manifested a religious sensitivity that outgrew the common practices of the Meccan people. He loved solitude and developed the habit of periodically withdrawing from human society to engage in meditation.

When Muhammad was about forty, he had a series of experiences that were to transform his life and inaugurate the public phase of his career. He began to receive revelations in the form of a voice and a vision. At first these experiences troubled him greatly, causing him to fear for himself and to despair. On

From a Qur'an manuscript, about 1300 A.D., with red highlights and gold leaf. The Maghribi style of script developed in the Maghrib (now Morocco, Algeria, Tunisia and Libya) and Spain. Photo: all rights reserved, The Metropolitan Museum of Art, Rogers Fund, 1942 (42. 63).

hearing about his revelations, Khadija and her cousin, Waraqa, a Christian, comforted and encouraged Muhammad. After sharing what had happened to him with others of his closely knit family, he began to gather a little group of sympathetic hearers about him. As he did so, other revelations came in the form of short messages, which he transmitted to his companions. For a long time the circle of sympathizers was limited to Muhammad's family and friends. Little in this quiet beginning presaged the emergence of a new world religion.

At this point it will be helpful to note something of the content of the messages Muhammad received. The themes of his early preaching were not extensive, but they were expressed with singular force. God's existence was taken for granted. The name given to God was Allah, a name not unknown to the Arabs. In fact, they considered Allah to be the high god of the many divinities they worshiped. The other gods were not immediately denied by Muhammad, but they were simply ignored. The Prophet proclaimed Allah (God) as the Creator, the source of life, the Lord of the Resurrection and the One who some day will call all human beings to account. We see these beliefs in some short extracts from the early revelations granted to the Prophet, which are recorded in the Muslim Scripture, the Qur'an.

Truly your Lord is the All-Wise Creator! (Sura "Al-Hijr," No. 15, verse 86)

Truly God is bountiful toward humankind, although most people do not give thanks. . . . God is the one who provided the earth as the place of your abode and the sky as an edifice, who formed you in suitable shapes and provided you with good things. (Sura "The Believer," No. 40, verses 61, 64)

When the trumpet sounds a single blast, and the earth and the mountains are lifted up and destroyed with a single blow, then that will be the eventful day. . . . On that day everything about you will be brought to light; no secret of yours will be concealed. (Sura "The Inevitable," No. 69, verses 13-15, 18)

Say: God gives you life, then causes you to die, and then gathers you on the day of resurrection. There is no doubt about this, although most people know nothing of it. (Sura "Kneeling," No. 45, verse 26)

The reference to ingratitude in the second quotation is a key to the further development of Muhammad's preaching to the Meccans. In addition to resounding warnings about the coming day of judgment when all people would have to account for their deeds, the message added that a life of trust in the Creator God should be one of constant gratitude for all of the good things of life.

> *But God you must serve and be among the thankful ones.* (Sura "The Groups," No. 39, verse 66)

One of the main ways to show gratitude and to demonstrate the reality of faith in God is to give of one's substance to help the needy.

> *So do your best to follow God, give heed, obey and be generous. That is best for you. Those who are saved from greed are the truly prosperous.* (Sura "Mutual Deception," No. 64, verse 16)

> *Whatever you give to the needy will be increased many times, if you do so in an attitude of seeking God's face.* (Sura "The Romans," No. 30, verse 39)

People from outside the Prophet's family gradually began to accept his message, but the population of Mecca in general did not welcome it. Perhaps the main factor in this rejection was that Muhammad was disturbing the established order of religious and commercial life. Urban Mecca bore within it the seeds of social disintegration, a situation common to cities where family ties were giving way to economic competition and social responsibility losing out to the individual's quest to get ahead. Muhammad's call to socially responsible behavior based on faith in a living, Creator God and a life lived in the immediate awareness of divine judgment clashed with the Meccans' sense of priorities and propriety.

Opposition to the Prophet and his followers arose in several forms. At one point the Meccans actually attacked them while they were gathered in a ravine outside the city to worship God. More often, though, the little group had to suffer abusive comments, ostracism and petty annoyances from their fellow citizens.

Around the year 615, five years after Muhammad's revelations, the pressure on those in Mecca who worshiped one God alone became so intense that about one hundred of them moved temporarily to the neighboring Christian country of Ethiopia, across the Red Sea from Arabia (as related on page 1). There they were sympathetically received until they returned to their homeland some years later.

After the year 619, the position of Muhammad and his followers in Mecca became more and more difficult. Khadija died, as did Muhammad's beloved uncle, Abu Talib. The number of Muslims, as the members of the little group were called, did not increase, and Muhammad's family became less and less supportive of him. Finally, help came from another locality, an oasis called Yathrib, more than two hundred miles north of Mecca. This was the home area of Muhammad's mother's family. In 620, men from Yathrib came to a fair in Mecca and were moved by the message of Islam. The next year and the next they brought others with them. On the third occasion, in 622, sev-

---

Muhammad's Family
After Khadija's death and in the course of the last thirteen years of his life, Muhammad married a number of times, according to the custom of his people. These polygamous unions were usually made with widows or divorced women and served the purpose both of providing needed protection for such women in the society of the time and of cementing political alliances with important leaders of Arabia. One of the best-remembered of Muhammad's wives was the young woman Aisha, who contributed a great deal to the record of the traditions of the Prophet.

Aisha herself, despite her young age [she was about eighteen when Muhammad died] was a living example of how prominent Arab women stood firm on many issues in those days. She was well known for her strong will and incisive logic and eloquence. She wielded a powerful intelligence which sometimes was even a match for the inspired and gifted Prophet of Allah.... She expressed her thoughts with a forthright and incisive logic and one day [Muhammad], while seated in the midst of other men, pointed towards her and said, "Draw half of your religion from this red one." She fought in several wars and battles, and was actively involved in politics and cultural and literary activities to such a degree that the theologian ... Orwa Ebn El Zobeir said: "I have not seer anyone who is more knowledgeable in theology, in medicine and in poetry than Aisha." (Quoted from *The Hidden Face of Eve: Women in the Arab World*, by Nawal El Saadawi (Boston: Beacon Press, 1982); © 1980 by Nawal El Saadawi.

enty-five men came to Mecca to pledge their support of Muhammad and to invite him, along with the Meccan believers, to live
in Yathrib.

This invitation set off a notable series of events that changed
the center of Muslim activity from Mecca to Yathrib, later known
as Medina. These events make up what Muslims call the
emigration, or *hijra*, and are considered the turning point in the
early history of Islam. Muslims begin their calendar at this
point, so that the year 622 A.D. corresponds to the first year of
the Islamic era.

About seventy Muslims made the journey north to take up
residence in Medina. Their Prophet became the leader of a
disparate, scattered population that had been weakened by years
of fighting between clans and factions, and he undertook to
mold a viable community based on the faith of Islam. The
inhabitants of Medina were for the most part non-nomadic
farmers, but the introduction of Meccan city dwellers into the
area increased the potential for economic development. Most
Medinans rallied to the side of their new leader, many in sincere
faith and others merely from self-interest. However, a large
number of the Jewish people in Medina refused to cooperate
with the Muslims and actually plotted to overthrow Muhammad. Their opposition was one of the first serious obstacles the
Muslims encountered in their new setting.

In Medina, conflicts continued on a larger scale than in
Mecca, but gradually, over the course of a decade, the Muslims
emerged victorious. They executed or banished the recalcitrant
Medinans, engaged the Meccans in battle, and extended their
influence to other areas of the Arabian Peninsula. Military
victories—and defeats—although painful and violent, were
occasions for the community to understand and express its
identity.

While actively and persuasively imposing his authority on the
populations of Arabia, Muhammad was busy erecting in Medina
the foundation of Muslim society. Responding to the revelatory
messages that he continued to receive, he taught that Islam was
an *umma*, or people, a society based not on blood ties but on
the ties of faith. The weak and the oppressed were to be
protected and liberated. Woman's position in relation to man's
was elevated. Laws of inheritance, of taxation, of warfare and
of social welfare initiated by the Prophet all moved toward a
broad and inclusive program of justice.

Tribes from far away sent delegations to Medina to negotiate their submission to the Prophet's authority. Muhammad wrote letters to other tribes and sent armed bands or delegations to seek their allegiance. A group of fourteen Christians, including a bishop, came from the Christian Arab city of Najran. After a discussion of their religious differences, the Christians agreed to accept Muhammad's political control; in return they were free to practice their Christian faith. They even asked Muhammad to send one of his men to Najran to arbitrate some difficult financial problems they were having.

By the year 631 much of the Arabian Peninsula had been united under Islam, including the city of Mecca, which had initially rejected Muhammad. Conditions were set for a wider expansion of the Islamic sphere of influence. However, Muhammad did not live to see this development. After making a pilgrimage to Mecca in the spring of 632, he succumbed to a disease, perhaps malaria, and died, at the age of sixty-two.

Thus we see that the man, Muhammad, was a basic factor in the foundation of Islam. And yet the Prophet Muhammad never claimed to be more than a messenger of God. According to Muslim belief he was a "warner" to call men and women from lives of foolish unbelief and vanity to sober faithfulness in the way of the living God. In the judgment of historians he was a remarkable leader and a wise statesman who spearheaded one of the most significant social revolutions in history. To Muslims he was the last and greatest of the Prophets of God.

The Scriptural Factor: The Qur'an

The third basic factor in the foundation of Islam is the book that Muslims believe to be God's revealed Word transmitted by the Prophet Muhammad. The name of the book, Qur'an—sometimes written less precisely as Koran—means literally, "recitation." The Qur'an contains the messages delivered, or recited, by Muhammad and gathered together by his followers into a book. The task of collecting the messages began even during the Prophet's lifetime

When translated from the original Arabic, the Qur'an is not an easy book to read. To appreciate its contents, non-Muslims need some guidance in approaching it. To the uninitiated its form can be mystifying. The text itself contains innumerable allusions, unusually concise expressions, renderings that read awkwardly in English, and obscure words. Linguistic and explanatory notes are needed if the translation is to be read with

The Caliphate at Its Greatest Extent

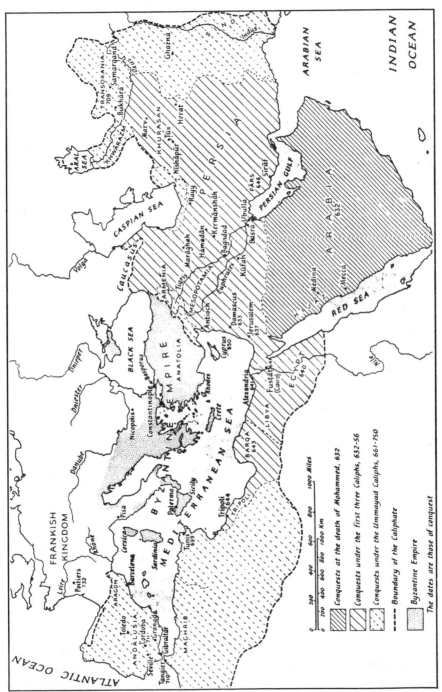

Conquests at the death of Mohammed, 632
Conquests under the first three Caliphs, 632–56
Conquests under the Ummayad Caliphs, 661–750
Boundary of the Caliphate
Byzantine Empire
The dates are those of conquest

understanding. Although no one translation of the Qur'an is entirely satisfactory, some good English translations exist and are available in inexpensive editions. Three of the most accessible versions are: *The Meaning of the Glorious Koran*, translated by Mohammad Marmaduke Pickthall; *The Holy Qur'an*, translated by Yusuf Ali, and *The Koran Interpreted*, translated by A.J. Arberry.

According to Muslim belief, throughout the ages God revealed his word to humankind through prophets by means of scripture. Before Muhammad, they believe, revelations had been given to various peoples, including the Hebrews through their prophet Moses and the Christians through their prophet, Jesus. The Qur'an, given as the culmination and conclusion of all previous prophetic revelations, was addressed to a people, the Arabs, who had not previously received a revelation in the Arabic language.

The vehicle of this final revelation was the language, Arabic, not the man, Muhammad, nor the event of Muhammad's call to prophethood. The essential role of the language means that *what* God said is inseparable from the *way* (through a particular language) the thoughts are expressed. So the meaning of the Qur'an cannot be conveyed exactly in any words other than the original Arabic words of the Book. From this conviction comes Muslims' feeling that no translation of the Qur'an is satisfactory. However, because so many languages exist in the world and so few people have the opportunity to learn Arabic, the use of translations of the Qur'an is accepted as necessary.

Muslims hold that Muhammad was the passive receiver of the revelation. The eternal words of God were transmitted to the Prophet by the angel Gabriel over a period of twenty-three years in varied circumstances. Although expressed in Arabic for the first time, the words themselves were not new. Muslims believe that they were taken from a well-guarded tablet in heaven, from which previous revelations to other peoples had also been taken. So in its essential content, the Qur'an is believed to be in agreement with the *Torah*, or Book of Moses, and the *Injil*, or Book of Jesus.*

---

* *Torah* and *Injil* are Arabic words. As used here, *Torah* does not refer directly to the Pentateuch of the Hebrew Scriptures, nor does *Injil* refer directly to the Greek Scriptures (the entire New Testament or the four Gospels contained in it). To Muslims, *Torah* and *Injil* are rather the revelations that God gave to Jews and Christians, revelations that no longer exist on earth in their pristine, original written forms.

The scripture of the Muslims is arranged in chapters called suras. Because the suras are mentioned in the Qur'an itself, they form a part of the original revelation. For example, one text says, "And when a sura is revealed. . ." (Sura "Repentance," No. 9, verse 86). Together the 114 suras form a book about the same length as the New Testament. On the whole, the suras are arranged in order of decreasing length. Each one is regarded as independent of the others, although scholars have seen significance in the order of their arrangement for interpreting the Book. The suras have titles, and it is by their names, rather than by their numbers, that they are most often known. The name is often a catchword found near the beginning of the sura; for example, "The Tidings" is the name of Sura 78. Other names may refer to some subject treated, such as "The Pilgrimage," Sura 22.

Every sura except Sura 9 begins with a prayer of invocation: "In the name of God, the Merciful, the Compassionate." Twenty-nine suras have three or four isolated Arabic letters at the beginning. Many theories have been advanced as to the meaning of these letters. They may be abbreviations. Some think they represent a mystery known only to God.

The suras are divided into verses, which form part of the structure of the text, unlike the Bible, where the verse division was an addition imposed on the text. These smaller divisions carry the evocative name of *aya*, meaning "sign" as well as "verse." So the verses of the Qur'an are signs of the mercy of God who reveals the message.

The language of the Qur'an is a rhymed prose; its verses rhyme but are not metrical. The text is recited on public occasions according to the requirements of a refined art of pronunciation and intonation.

To understand the Qur'an we must first distinguish between suras referring to the Meccan period of Muhammad's life and those referring to the Medinan period. The heading of each sura indicates whether, in the opinion of Muslim scholarship, it was revealed in Mecca or in Medina. The Meccan suras are usually short, although the later ones increase in length. They deal with the fundamental content of Muslim faith. The Medinan suras speak of events in the early history of Islam and set forth laws and principles for the good order of the community.

The Qur'an refers to many events that are recounted in the Bible and mentions a number of the Biblical patriarchs, kings and prophets, such as Adam, Abraham, Isaac, Jacob, Job, Solomon, David, Joseph, Moses, Aaron, Zachariah, John the Baptist, Elijah, Ishmael, Elisha, Jonah and Lot. Jesus and the Virgin Mary also figure prominently in the text.

The Qur'an is not a book of history, although historical events form the background of its messages. It is a vast collection of warnings, exhortations, discourses, allegorical sayings, formulas of worship, prescriptions, prayers and descriptive passages.

Neither is the Qur'an a theological treatise. The work of systematizing the faith of Islam was given to heirs of the Book in later centuries. To Muslims the Qur'an is the record of how God spoke through Muhammad to warn all people, to summon them to repentance and faith and to clarify their duty. So the Book contains the divine principles that should direct the personal and social life of humanity. Together with the traditions (*hadith*) of the Prophet, it provides the source of doctrine and of ethics.

Finally, the Qur'an is the principal book of liturgy for Islamic worship. Sura No. 1, "The Opener," is used at every time of prayer. Muslims draw their main spiritual nourishment from the sounds and meanings of their Scripture. In their view, the Book is also the source of the truest and best education. Studies in grammar, philology, literature, elocution and law all take their primary inspiration from the Glorious Qur'an.

It is not possible for non-Muslims who lack a knowledge of Arabic to appreciate the power and impact of the Qur'an, because its content and manner of expression are quite inseparable. Nevertheless, one who reads the text in translation can get some hint of its syntactical force, gripping imagery, moving appeal and sheer beauty. If you want to read the Qur'an in translation, some suggestions may prove helpful. It is better not to try to read straight through the text. Begin, rather, with some shorter suras, such as "The Resurrection," No. 75; "The Cleaving," No. 82; "The Cloaked One," No. 84; "The Morning Hours," No. 93; "The Evening," No. 103; "The Unbelievers," No. 109 and "Sincerity," No. 112. Try to grasp the thrust of each sura as a whole. Pay attention to sequences of thought, repetitions, refrains, references to historical persons and events, dramatic structure (who speaks and who is addressed), figures of speech, descriptions of creation and of the hereafter, commands, exhortations, promises and warnings. As you gain some familiarity with short suras, move on to such longer, more complex ones as "Mary," No. 19; "The Spider," No. 29 and "The Merciful," No. 55.

The various styles of the Arabic calligraphy of the Qur'an inspired design of many arts, from architecture to glass, metal, embroidery and others. Objects in daily use were included in this artistry, thus reminding the user of the unity as well as the beauty of life under God. This pottery plate was made in Persia (now Iran) in the late tenth century A.D.

The Doctrinal Factor: Confession of Faith

The beliefs of Islam can be found in the Qur'an, but not arranged in systematic order. Muslim scholars have systematized the doctrines, and in every period of history they have produced many books dealing with the content of their faith. A remarkable variety of books and articles is being published in many languages to explain and comment on the beliefs of Islam as Muslims understand them today. Muslims have made great use of the catechism method of religious education, presenting doctrines to students in the form of questions and answers.

In this book, we do not have space to survey the whole field of doctrinal development. Instead, in the few paragraphs devoted to doctrine as an element in the foundation of Islam, I shall comment on the central confession of faith, the recitation of which is perhaps the most fundamental act of Muslims everywhere. No other statement sums up so clearly and succinctly what Muslims believe. The whole subject of theology is epitomized in these few words, upon whose meanings Islam was founded.

To begin, we look in the Qur'an. Sura 47, "Muhammad," verse 19, says, "So, know that there is no deity except God and ask forgiveness for your sin. . . ." Then in the following sura, No. 48, "Victory," verse 29, it is said, "Muhammad is the messenger of God. . . ." These two affirmations were joined in a confession of faith, or creed, called "The Witness" *(shahada)* of the community and of each individual within the community. Muslims say, "I witness that there is no deity except God, and I witness that Muhammad is the messenger of God."

The first half of this short creed fulfils two functions: it rejects all other gods, be they idols, spirits, phenomena of nature, creatures of the earth or philosophical inventions of the mind ("... there is no deity..."), and it affirms the reality of the true God (". . . except God"). The one, the only God in Islam is unique in life, power, mercy and justice. In solitary majesty God has no partner in creation, no equal or even likeness in perfection, no sharer in receiving the worship of earthborn creatures and heavenly beings. God is understood as the only final cause of everything in the universe, regardless of how many intricate secondary causes may be discovered by science. God is only good, so only good can ultimately come to trusting human beings, in spite of the pain that may be encountered along the way

Belief in the uniqueness of God is a practical doctrine because it results in a serene and single-minded life, relieving the believer of excessive preoccupation with passing circumstances and conditions of life. Muslims live in the immediate consciousness of the luminous reality of God as close at hand, but at the same time exalted over all creation. One of the first Muslims is

---

Praise to the Transcendent God

A prayer in a Shi'a breviary, attributed to Ali Zain al-Abidin:
O Thou who art described though no description reaches thy True Being, nor does any deliminator draw limits for Thee. Thou who art absent from us in mystery yet not lost, Thou Seer who art not seen, Thou who art sought and found, for neither the heavens nor the earth nor the intervening space is void of Thee for the flicker of an eyelid. Thou art not liable to modality nor susceptible of spaciality or localization. Thou art the Light of Light and Lord of Lords encompassing all things. Glory to Him whom nothing resembles, the All-Hearer, the All-Seer. Glory to Him who is thus and no other is thus.

From *Muslim Devotions: A Study of Prayer Manuals in Common Use*, © Constance Padwick (1961); reproduced by permission of SPCK, London.

said to have declared by faith, "God is both outside all things and inside all things: outside, but not alien to them; inside, but not identical with them." Muslims owe allegiance only to God. A divided allegiance denies the perfect divine oneness. No sin in Islam is greater than to associate anything, any person, any ideal or any affection, with God in loyalty and devotion. To commit that sin is to violate the integrity of authentic life, which is meant to reflect the oneness of its Creator.

The second half of the creed ("... and I witness that Muhammad is the messenger of God") affirms the prophethood of Muhammad. His role is derived from the broader doctrine of prophets, which is, next to belief in the one God, the most important belief of Islam. According to this conviction, throughout history God has granted the gracious gift of guidance to the peoples of the earth through the intermediary of prophets. In the following summary of the doctrine of prophets, I draw on material in an old catechism used for Muslim religious education.

In Islam, prophets are human messengers whom God has mercifully sent in order to explain to other human beings their duty toward God and one another, to announce rewards for those who do good and to warn of punishment for those who do evil. Prophets make known the realities that are normally hidden from human sight, things that human thought cannot attain without divine help. Some prophets, such as Moses, Jesus and Muhammad, were given Scriptures, and Muslims believe in

---

A Prayer for Readers of the Qur'an

A prayer from a prayerbook by Ali Muhammad al-Qari (the book was bought in Cairo):

Increase our longing for it [the Word of God in the Qur'an]; multiply our delight in it, to the number of the raindrops and the leaves on the trees. Through it, perfect our confidence in the guidance of the good and the glad tidings of men of spiritual experience. Bring to our minds what we have forgotten of it. Teach us what we do not know of its radiant truths and secret touches of meaning. Make it for us an *imam* and light and guidance and mercy in the abode below and the abode everlasting. And grant us the reading of it in the hours of night and the seasons of the day.

From *Muslim Devotions,* © Constance Padwick (1961); reproduced by permission of SPCK, London.

all books given to prophets. No one knows how many prophets there have been. The first one was Adam, and the last one was Muhammad. Twenty-five are named in the Qur'an. Among these are Noah, Abraham, Lot, Ishmael, Isaac, Jacob, Job, Moses, Aaron, David, Solomon, Elijah, Elisha, Jonah, Zachariah, John the Baptist and Jesus.

Prophets were chosen because of their exceptional character as fitting transmitters of the divine commands and ordinances to humankind. They did not differ from one another in their essential messages, since what they brought was true religion and what they instilled was faith. There can be no multiplicity or variation in faith and true religion, Muslims believe. If prophets differed, they differed in certain details of practice, which naturally varied according to the era, location, and situation in which people lived, as well as according to peoples' cultural and ethnic backgrounds.

Muhammad was the seal of the prophets, meaning that after him no other prophet would come. He lived the best of lives, ever faithful to his family, helpful to the needy, enduring in the face of trial, persevering in the tasks he had to perform, indulgent, kind and gentle toward others. He spent much time in silent meditation on the secrets of God's kingdom. He spoke rarely, but when he did speak it was with clarity and at times with humor. He was utterly truthful and humble. At the same time he inspired awe in his companions, who by following him attained the highest level of intellectual and moral virtue. Even those of his contemporaries who did not follow him were influenced by his achievements. Muhammad was the noblest of creatures in both his inner and his outer qualities.

From the two fundamental doctrines announced in the creed, belief in the one God and belief in prophets, derive such other beliefs as faith in divinely revealed Scriptures, the resurrection, the day of judgment and the life hereafter. Muslims have pondered these great truths extensively and discussed their varying interpretations of them, but theological discussion as such—that is, speculation and investigation of the doctrines alone—has not been the principal activity of religious scholars. The religion of Muslims has made them extremely practical people. They concentrate on the precise duties of believers and on efforts to create a good life for the community more than on doctrinal discussion. We shall look at these duties and efforts in the next chapter, on Islamic Patterns of Life.

3

Islamic Patterns of Life

*T*he duty of Muslims is clear in its broad outline. There is no need for misunderstanding or hesitation in living the life prescribed for them, a life of serious purpose and of social responsibility. The principles for daily living are contained in the Qur'an and the authoritative traditions of the Prophet Muhammad, which point out the example that he set for human life. These traditions, called *hadith*, number several thousand and have been transmitted by faithful authorities through the centuries from one generation to another, beginning with the men and women who actually knew Muhammad.

The directives for proper conduct contained in the two sources, Qur'an and hadith, make up what is called the *shari'a* and form a flexible and comprehensive guide for personal and social ethics, and an explanation of how to render worthy and disciplined worship to Almighty God. Sometimes the shari'a is called religious law, but that term is somewhat too narrow for the scope of the prescriptions contained in the sources. Many books have been written and schools of thought formed concerning the interpretation and application of the shari'a. These are not the shari'a itself, but rather writings and schools of jurisprudence, or, in Arabic, *fiqh*.

For the sake of classification and rational analysis, the prescriptions of the law are divided into two categories: duties of worship and duties of human relationships. This division does not correspond to the traditional Western distinction between sacred and secular duties, because in the fundamental vision of Islam, life is a unified whole under the one God. All duties are religious duties, in the broad, inclusive sense. For example, to make a business contract is just as much an act of faith as to say a prayer. (But later we shall see that this indivisible view of life in Islam is being severely tested in many countries today by the pervasive forces of secularization.)

Duties of Worship

The duties of worship are commonly described as five in number, the famous five pillars of Islam.

1. Confession of faith
2. Prayer
3. Contribution to charity
4. Fasting during the month of Ramadan
5. Pilgrimage to Mecca — one time require, Released from requir if finan hardsh etc.

We shall look at these duties in some detail because they constitute much of what is unique about Islam.

1. Confession of Faith

The end of Chapter 2 described the Islamic creed, or confession of faith, as "the doctrinal factor." This chapter on "Patterns of Life" begins with a discussion of the same subject, the confession of faith. By this arrangement I want to show how closely Muslims link faith and life, doctrine and practice. The first "pillar" of Islamic *practice* is also the primary statement of *doctrine*: the confession of belief in God and the messenger of God, Muhammad. This strikingly direct formula, with its expression of personal involvement ("I witness . . ."), its strong rejection of false gods (". . . there is no deity . . ."), its ringing affirmation of the exclusive place of the one God (". . . except God") and its statement of the key role of Muhammad in all that is Islamic (". . . Muhammad is the messenger of God") is the key to admission into the community of Islam. Children of Muslims are born into the orbit of active faith and grow up nurtured in the two tenets of the creed, God's oneness and Muhammad's prophethood. Islam has no rite of passage whereby children pass from a state of not being Muslims into the fellowship of the community.* Here is more evidence of the inclusiveness of Islam: it embraces Muslim children from the time of their birth.

The act of saying the creed is in itself a part of faith. Muslims define the act of faith as the conviction of the heart, the testimony of the lips and deeds of righteousness. Different schools of thought have emphasized one or more of these three elements, but the first pillar, confession of faith, is always consid-

---

* Although not mentioned in the Qur'an or the hadith, circumcision is practiced in Islam. Indeed, circumcision is regarded as essential in being a (male) Muslim, but it is *not* a condition or sign of entry into Islam.

ered a part of the act of believing. The faithful repeat this testimony several times each day of their lives. It provides a stabilizing orientation for all their activities. To repeat it is to invoke the power and mercy of God in all the demands that life makes upon human beings.

2. Prayer

Muslims are people of prayer. Their religious law sets five times each day when they should devote a few minutes to the praise and adoration of God. This prescription is not optional, so no Muslim has to choose the best time to pray. At dawn, at noon, in midafternoon, at sunset and in the night, members of the worldwide community are called to prostrate themselves before their Lord in acts of humble obedience, in communion with the One whom they call the Merciful, and in the desire to combat through prayer the human inclination toward evil. Someone once asked the Prophet, "Which (human) deed is most precious to God?" He replied, "Prayer performed at the proper time."

Because the Islamic prayer cycle is based on the rising and setting of the sun, the hours for prayer change with the seasons of the year. Newspapers and calendars in Muslim countries print the times for each day of the year.

Before praying, believers prepare themselves thoughtfully and deliberately by a ceremonial washing of the face and limbs. This washing has both literal and symbolic meaning. It is essential to be clean, both outwardly and inwardly, before going to God in prayer. Bodily functions and physical contact with certain substances are considered to cause physical and ceremonial uncleanness and to require worshipers to perform ablutions. But worshipers are also required to seek the cleansing of their inner selves by confession to God and repentance. An ancient master of the faith wrote, "Praise be to God, who has bestowed kindness upon us, and has invited us to cleanliness; who has granted light and grace for the purification of our inward thoughts and who, for the washing of our bodies, has given pure, soothing water." As a precaution against perfunctory ablution, the Prophet is quoted as saying, "Those who remember God when they perform their ablutions will have their whole body purified by God. But those who do not remember God at ablutions will not be purified except in those places where the water was applied."

The call to prayer is itself an act of worship, an exclamation of praise. This invitation is not required for the valid performance of prayer, but it is always practiced in populated areas,

A worshiper in prayer in the historic Shah mosque on the Royal Square in Isfahan, Iran. United Nations photo, PB/jr.

often chanted in a melodious tone from the tower of the place of worship, or *mosque.* The wording of the call varies slightly in different parts of the Muslim world, but in most places it contains the following elements:

> *"God is great!"* (said two or four times)
> *"I witness that there is no deity except God."*
> (repeated)
> *"I witness that Muhammad is the messenger of God."*
> (repeated)
> *"Come to prayer."* (repeated)
> *"Come to the good life."* (repeated)
> (at the dawn prayer only) *"Prayer is better than sleep."*
> *"God is great!"* (repeated)
> *"There is no deity except God."*

In response to the call, the worshipers proceed to the act of prayer, the central act of worship for all of the Muslim world, and perhaps the most characteristic mark of Islam. The prayer is composed of a series of postures, gestures, recitations and periods of silence. Facing in the direction of Mecca, the worshipers quietly announce to themselves their intention to perform *salat,* as the ritual prayer is called. They stand as they begin the act, then bend the body so that the hands touch the knees. After rising again to a standing position, they kneel and then bring their heads down to touch the ground. Finally, they rest quietly on their knees, sitting on their feet. This sequence of positions is followed two, three or four times, depending on the time of day. During salat the worshipers must not converse or look around. Forbidden are any gestures or words not authorized by the religious law. At each of the positions certain words are said. Aside from requests for mercy, pardon and guidance, almost all of the prayer words are expressions of praise and adoration of God. The first sura of the Qur'an is always recited at each prayer period. The words of this sura, named "The Opener," are:

> *In the name of God, the Merciful, the Compassionate.*
> *Praise be to God, the Lord of the Worlds,*
> *The Merciful, the Compassionate,*
> *Master of the Day of Judgment.*
> *You we worship; you we ask for help.*
> *Guide us in the straight path,*
> *The path of those whom you have blessed,*
> *Not the path of those who have incurred your wrath,*
> *Nor of those who have gone astray.*

Besides "The Opener," worshipers recite other passages from the Qur'an, chosen according to their particular circumstances or personal needs and desires.

Prayer may be said in any convenient place, either individually or in a group. On Fridays at the noon prayer time, Muslims gather at the mosque for communal worship and a sermon. A mosque can be either a simple room set aside for worship in a building used for other purposes or a large structure dedicated entirely to the communal practice of prayer and to the teaching of Islam. The furnishings of a mosque are simple in the extreme. No chairs or benches are needed, because the congregation stands and kneels for prayer. People leave their shoes at the door of the mosque, because the floor is kept clean. It is covered by carpets or mats, on which the worshipers sit while listening to the preacher or to the one intoning the Qur'an, or while they meditate individually. Other furnishings include bookcases for copies of the Qur'an and a pulpit for the preacher on Friday.

Every mosque has a large niche built into the wall on the side of the building that faces Mecca. This focal point for the act of worship may be ornamented with stuccowork, but is unfurnished. No pictures or carvings of living creatures are seen anywhere in the mosque. Images are forbidden so as to avoid any suggestion of idol worship.

The leaders of the services at the mosque are not clergy in the Christian sense. There is no priesthood in Islam, nor is there a function to correspond to that of the Protestant minister. Any members of the Muslim community can serve as prayer leaders, preachers and teachers, provided that they have the necessary training and that their devotion and good character are recognized by the community.

The five times of salat each day do not exhaust Muslims' opportunities for prayer. Living as they do in the intense consciousness of God's power and presence, many find occasions for calling upon God by praise and supplication in the various circumstances of everyday life. Free, optional prayer is called by a different name than ritual prayer. Models for this type of prayer are often drawn from the hadith, which preserve a large number of the Prophet's own supplications and expressions of praise. Free prayer requires no set time, but finds its natural setting in the ongoing flow of daily events, whether ordinary or extraordinary. Some of the moments that call forth this kind of prayer are awakening in the morning, leaving the house, entering the mosque, finishing the ritual prayer, going to market,

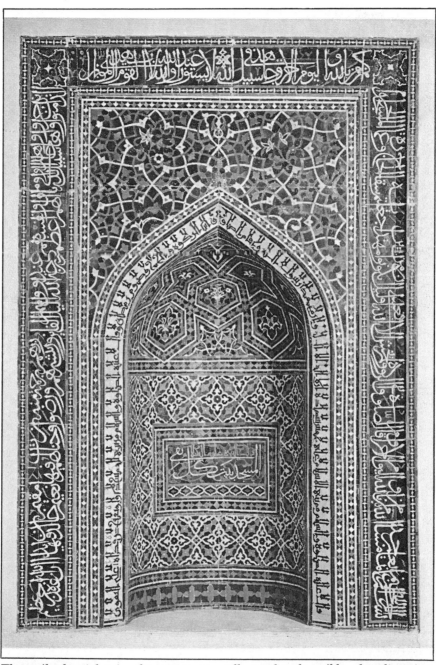

The *mihrab,* niche in the mosque wall, marks the *qibla,* the direction of Mecca. This elaborate niche of glazed earthenware mosaic was in the Madrasa Imami in Isfahan, Iran, built in 1354 A.D. Photo: all rights reserved, The Metropolitan Museum of Art, Harris Brisbane Dick Fund, 1939. (39.20).

dressing, reflecting on debts to pay, seeing the new moon, observing the phenomena of wind, rain and thunder, hearing of someone's death, feeling angry or fearful, and suffering distress, pain or grief.

3. Contribution to Charity

In Islam, faith influences believers' attitude toward material possessions. God is the Creator and owner of all things. People are entrusted with varying amounts of wealth to be used to satisfy their needs and to help others. The possession of wealth involves the particular responsibility to use it unselfishly. As an institutional expression of this stewardship of material goods, Muslims are required each year to contribute about two and one-half percent of the value of their wealth to care for those who are poor and otherwise unfortunate. They do not consider this duty to be a tax, but rather an act of worship.

Besides providing an effective safeguard against the evils of abject poverty, contributing to the poor is interpreted as having various spiritual benefits. In the Qur'an it is said that believers will be tested by God in their possessions and in their persons (Sura "The Family," No. 3, verse 186). The required contribution to charity is seen as one way of experiencing that testing. In this way the givers develop goodness in themselves and a measure of detachment from their possessions. Also, the wealth retained grows in value by becoming more of an asset than if it were kept entirely in a selfish spirit. When used by faith, wealth helps its possessors to gain a particular recompense from God, both in this life and in the life to come.

The Arabic name for this pillar sums up its religious significance: *zakat*, from a root meaning "to grow, increase," and "to be pure." By practicing zakat Muslims believe that their wealth is increased in value, and that they and their wealth are purified. In many countries the paying of zakat is left to the consciences of individual Muslims. In others the government collects the amount due. In this practice we see a good example of the uniting of devotional and social aspects of life in the way of Islam.

4. Fasting During the Month of Ramadan

For an entire month each year Muslims are required to abstain completely from eating and drinking during daylight hours. *Ramadan* is the name of the month that is devoted to fasting. During the time of abstinence, daily work normally continues as usual, although the community is tolerant toward those who give in to lassitude during the month. Each believer is expected to perform supplementary prayers during Ramadan and to take part in special ceremonies at the mosque.

In a Muslim country the authorities provide public signals of various kinds to mark the beginning and the end of the fast each day. People are awakened early enough each morning to eat a meal just before the break of day. At sunset food is eaten almost immediately, either just before or just after the sunset prayer. Each region of the Muslim world has particular items of food that are habitually eaten to break the fast. Later a more copious

---

The Islamic Calendar

The Islamic calendar is lunar. Each of the twelve months in the year begins with the appearance of the new moon. The months alternate in length between twenty-nine and thirty days. The dating of the Islamic calendar begins with the Holy Prophet Muhammad's flight (Hijra) from Mecca to Medina in 622 C.E. [Common Era; same as A.D.]. The years 1989-90 C.E. correspond to the years 1410/1411 A.H. ("the year of the Hijra"). While the several different Muslim communities have some holy days of their own, the principal holy days of the Islamic year are celebrated by all Muslims, regardless of their affiliation. Some dates for 1989 are:

Mar. 4: Miraj al-Nabi, the ascension of the Prophet, commemorates Muhammad's death in 632 C.E.

Apr. 7: The Holy Month of Ramadan begins. This is the ninth month of the year and is a month of fasting during which Muslims do not eat or drink from sunrise to sunset.

May 2: Laylat al-Qadr, the Night of Power, commemorates the first revelation of the Qur'an to Prophet Muhammad.

May 7: 'Id al-Fitr, the Festival of the Fast Breaking, celebrates the end of Ramadan.

July 13: 'Id al-Adha, the Festival of the Sacrifice, is in remembrance of the sacrifice of Abraham, his wife Hagar and their son Ishmael. It is a day related to the pilgrimage to Mecca.

Aug. 3: First of Muharram, the first month of the Islamic year 1410 A.H.

Aug. 12: Ashura is a day in memory of Imam Hussayn, the grandson of Prophet Muhammad.

Oct. 12: Mawlid al-Nabi is the anniversary of the birth of Prophet Muhammad.

Information from The Multifaith Calendar, by permission of the Multifaith Calendar Committee, Canadian Ecumenical Action, 1410 West 12th Ave., Vancouver, BC, V6H 1M8.

meal is served. Often the nights of Ramadan are spent in social visiting and entertainment, as well as in exercises of religious devotion.

The fast, instituted in the second year of the Muslim era, is considered a duty that is pleasing to God. It has both a physical side—total abstinence from food and drink—and a moral side— refraining from forbidden words and deeds. The Prophet Muhammad said, "If you do not give up lying there is no need for you to give up eating and drinking." The fast is not considered valid if the person observing it entertains thoughts of envy or hatred.

In principle, the idea of ascetic denial of the pleasure of the flesh is absent from Muslim fasting. Instead, emphasis is placed on the discipline of character that fasting encourages. It is said that fasting educates the will and the conscience by refusing the body its habitual and selfish requirements. It is believed that fasting physically strengthens the digestive system and contributes to recovery from several diseases. Ramadan also puts the rich and the poor on the same level, at least temporarily, so that the rich should feel compassionate toward the poor.

Children begin to fast seriously at about the age of thirteen, although they may participate partially in the practice at an earlier age. Elderly people and those seriously ill are exempt from fasting. The sick, women during their menstrual period or in childbirth, pregnant women and nursing mothers, travelers under difficult circumstances and soldiers in battle are also exempt by virtue of their temporary circumstances, but they are expected to fast later in the year to make up for the time that they did not fast during Ramadan.

Even when we begin to understand how the month of Ramadan is observed, we are still far from grasping the essence of this practice for Muslim devotion. To come to a sympathetic understanding of the fast requires sensitivity to the varied aspects of religious feeling in Islam. Some Muslims affirm that they never feel better, physically and mentally, than during the month of Ramadan. Others emphasize that it helps a believer to concentrate on the unremitting struggle against the baser tendencies of human nature. For some it symbolizes the willingness of Muslims to surrender to the will of God. Again, it is interpreted as one of the means whereby a Muslim communes with God and enters into the deep meaning of the divine message to humankind.

The fast is also a commemorative act, a manner of rendering

Prayer for the Twenty-Fourth Day of Ramadan

A prayer of 'Ali Zayin al-'Abidin, from a Shi'a prayerbook:
Praise be to Him who when I call on Him answers me, slow though
    I am when He calls me.
Praise be to Him who gives to me when I ask Him, miserly though
    I am when He asks a loan of me.
Praise be to Him to whom I confide my needs whensoever I will
    and He satisfies them.
My Lord I praise, for He is of my praise most worthy.

From: *Muslim Devotions,* © Constance Padwick (1961); reproduced
by permission of SPCK, London.

---

praise to God for two great historical events that are believed
to have taken place during the month of Ramadan. The first of
these was the beginning of the revelation of the Qur'an to
Muhammad. The second was the military victory at Badr, the
first great trial of the new community of believers formed in
Medina under Muhammad's leadership.

Muslims believe that fasting during Ramadan will insure the
pardon of their sins from one year to the next—provided, of
course, that the act of privation is done for God alone. In general,
Islam has not taught the concept of penitence or of atonement
for sin by suffering or deprivation. Thus, we should not let the
idea that fasting takes away sins lead us to conclude that Islam
is a religion teaching salvation through pious deeds. Such an
erroneous conclusion stems from judging Islam according to the
terms of Christian doctrine and the Christian way of thinking,
and only distorts the image of Islam. According to Islam, good
works such as prayer, fasting and almsgiving, when performed
with humility, meet the approval of God and gain merit for
those who do them, but ultimately salvation comes only from
God's power and mercy. The Prophet Muhammad said, "If you
go forth from your home, crying, 'I go out in the name of God,
putting my trust in Him, since there is no strength to resist evil
and no power to do good save through Him,' you will be
greeted with: 'You are guided, you have enough, you are saved,
and Satan will leave you alone.'"

Apart from the foregoing interpretations of and motivations
for fasting, most Muslims are content with the certainty that
because God has ordained the fast they must observe it. The
spirit of true devotion seeks no other reason for the act, no other

motivation. Ramadan provides a concrete and easily grasped means for maintaining a satisfactory relationship with the Creator.

Finally, the fast of Ramadan is a remarkable social phenomenon. Not only is it a forceful witness to faith by the entire community, but because it provides a definitive break in the ordinary run of life, Ramadan constitutes a refreshing and uplifting interlude for the masses, a time of diversion that is sanctioned by a severe discipline.

On the day after the end of Ramadan occurs one of the most important holidays of the Muslim calendar. In the intensity and enthusiasm with which it is celebrated, the *'Id al-Fitr*, as it is called, corresponds to the Christians' festival of Christmas, although the meanings of the two occasions are completely different. The name of the holiday means simply, "The Feast of the Breaking of the Fast," so its significance depends on the period of severe discipline to which the community submitted itself just prior to its celebration. The 'Id al-Fitr is a festival of victory and faith. It is a time of relaxation, of hope renewed, of strengthened resolution to do what is right, of good will toward all. The outward manifestations of these inner feelings consist of special prayers said as a group at the mosque, the wearing of new clothes, the distribution of food to the poor, the partaking of culinary delicacies, the giving of gifts to the children, reconciliation with any enemies and the renewal of ties of friendship and kinship. The outburst of joy and thankfulness occasioned by the 'Id al-Fitr lasts for several days.

5. Pilgrimage to Mecca

The fifth pillar of Islam requires that every Muslim make the journey to Mecca at least once in a lifetime, if economic circumstances permit. According to the Qur'an, the faith of Muslims is closely related to that of Abraham. The Scripture of Islam does not announce a new doctrine, but rather it recommends a return to the pure monotheistic faith of Abraham, who was called the "Friend of God."

When Muslims make the pilgrimage to Mecca, they find the Abrahamic elements of their religion brought to life for their imaginations. All pilgrims dress in similar white garments of ancient style to remind them of the time of Abraham. They do homage at the Ka'ba, the ancient shrine on the spot where they believe that Abraham built the first House of God. They walk seven times between two hills in the city in memory of Hagar, repudiated by Abraham, who is believed to have run back and

Worshipers in Mecca during the Hajj

The black, cube-shaped structure in the middle of the photograph is the Ka'ba, which contains a mass of meteorite material that had been venerated as a shrine by Arabs for centuries before Muhammad. Muhammad rededicated the shrine to God; the stone within it is to Muslims a sign of God's covenant with Abraham. In a ritual called *tawaf*, pilgrims walk around the Ka'ba three times during the Hajj; at the beginning, after the sacrifice, and before leaving Mecca. Those who are able to be close to the stone meditate near it and kiss it; others extend their arms toward it while reciting the pilgrim's prayer. The Ka'ba is the center toward which daily prayers are prayed.

Photo courtesy of the Information Office, Royal Embassy of Saudi Arabia, Washington, D.C.

forth there in search of water for herself and for her son, Ishmael. They draw water from the well of Zamzam, reputed to be the source of water miraculously provided for the mother and son. The multitudes of pilgrims throw stones at a masonry pillar in the Valley of Mina to commemorate Abraham's rejection of satanic temptations. Then on the tenth day of the month of Dhu al-Hijja, two months and ten days after the end of the fast of Ramadan, the pilgrims sacrifice an animal in memory of Abraham's willingness to sacrifice his son in obedience to the command of God.

The *Hajj*, or Pilgrimage to Mecca, is the most important manifestation of the worldwide community of Islam. In recent years, up to two million pilgrims have gathered for the ceremonies that take place during the first days of the month of Dhu al-Hijja. These people, coming from all parts of the earth and representing all classes and conditions of life, demonstrate in a striking way Islamic unity, a unity founded on the truth of God's absolute oneness. Together, regardless of language, race or background, they unite their voices in the famous cry of worship, *"Labbaika, Allahumma, labbaika"* (O God, here I am, at your service), uttered frequently and fervently as they proceed in a devotional spirit through the ceremonies of pilgrimage.

Elsewhere in the world of Islam, believers are in communion with the pilgrims, especially on the day of sacrifice. Every year the faithful observe the sacrifice in their own locality simultaneously with those in Mecca. The ceremony of sacrifice is called, in Arabic, the *'Id al-Adha* (The Festival of Sacrifice). Tradition prescribes a special communal prayer on the morning of the festival. After the prayer comes the moment of sacrifice, and tradition furnishes detailed instructions regarding which animals can be used, how they are to be slaughtered and the ways in which the flesh of the victim is to be used. Sheep are commonly offered as sacrificial animals, but camels, cattle and goats are also acceptable. Usually one animal is slaughtered for each household, although several families may join to sacrifice one animal. The head of the household offers this prayer, or a similar one, at the moment that the victim is killed:

> *O Lord, my God, receive the sacrifice of* (naming himself) *for himself, his spouse, his children and all of his family, which is made according to the example of our Lord Abraham (may peace be upon him).*

A Gift at 'Id al-Adha

In 1988 when Canadian Muslims celebrated the Festival of Sacrifice, they contributed part of the meat to food banks maintained by Christians to help the poor. The people of Canada were very pleased by this gift of $500,000 (Canadian) worth of meat, the first fresh meat ever given to the food banks. *RMS*

Part of the meat is eaten during the several days of festivities that follow the sacrifice and other portions are given to the poor. An atmosphere of serene joy pervades the community.

The ritual sacrifice has its origins in the Qur'an. The Qur'anic story of Abraham's sacrifice is not very different from that of the Bible, although it is less detailed. The Qur'an does not give the name of the son who was offered. However, Muslim tradition affirms that the son was Ishmael and not Isaac, as the Bible has it, and, further, that Ishmael married into the tribe of Meccan Arabs out of which the Prophet Muhammad arose.

Christians often ask whether the sacrifice of the 'Id al-Adha conveys a sense of expiation of sins. According to the most commonly accepted doctrine, there is no place in Islam for a blood sacrifice to expiate sin. The rites of pilgrimage, including the sacrifice, were instituted against a background of pre-Islamic religious practices in which sacrificial blood was shed to purify the worshiper from sin. But in Sura "The Pilgrimage," No. 22, we read about the Islamic nature of the ceremony to be observed at the time of the pilgrimage to Mecca. Believers are put on guard against a false interpretation of the sacrifice, influenced by pre-Islamic beliefs:

> *Neither their flesh [that of sacrificed animals] nor their blood will ever reach God; it is piety that will reach Him.* (verse 37)

So the expiatory sacrifice of pre-Islamic Arabs was replaced in Islam by a purely commemorative rite.

Yet anthropologists and other observers have noted that the generally accepted doctrine is often linked in the popular spirit of many Muslims with vestiges of archaic religion, which differs according to the region of the world in which the believers live. In several areas, local beliefs and practices, dating from before the Islamization of the population, emphasized expiatory sacrifice, and these beliefs continue to influence attitudes toward the Islamic rite of sacrifice. So some Muslims will say that the sacrifice of the 'Id al-Adha is an effective means of obtaining divine pardon of their sins.

More authentically Islamic lessons to be drawn from the example of Abraham are: that God will answer the prayers of sincere and faithful worshipers; that love of parents and obedience to them bring God's blessing; and that faith in the heart of a believer inspires him or her to sacrifice to God that which is most precious.

Duties of Human Relationships

The second broad category of duties for which the shari'a lays down the basic principles has to do with personal and social ethics. As we noted earlier, Islam is a system whose faith perspective integrates all aspects of life, so that the duties of human relationships are considered as religious duties just as much as are acts of worship.

Moral Values

As might be expected, the basis for moral values in Islam is found in the Qur'an. Doing good deeds and being of a good character are both considered responses of obedience to God by the person of faith. And to do evil is to disobey God. Here are some verses from the Qur'an that set up clear moral standards for those who follow its teachings in a spirit of commitment to the will and authority of God.

> *The servants of the All-Merciful One are they who go modestly upon the earth. When foolish people accost them they reply, "Peace!" They spend nights in prayer, standing and prostrate before their Lord. They say, "Save us from the suffering of hell, for it is a fearful torment, an evil place in which to abide." They are the ones who spend of their wealth, but in moderation, being neither extravagant nor niggardly. They cry out to no other deity than God. They take the life of no human being, unless to satisfy the demands of justice. They do not commit adultery, for those guilty of that act will pay the penalty; their doom will be doubled on the day of resurrection, and they will lie in the shame of torment forever, unless they repent and believe and do good deeds. If they repent God will change their evil deeds into good ones. God is all-forgiving, all-merciful. Whoever repents and does good turns to God in true contrition. The servants of God are those who do not gaze on vain things, but when they encounter temptation they pass by unsullied. When they are reminded of God's mercies toward them they are not unheeding. They say, "O Lord, give us joy in our spouses and children and make us an example to those who seek to follow you." These will be given a reward on high because they were steadfast and they will be gathered together with greetings of peace. They will*

remain there forever, in the blissful abiding place.
(Sura "The Criterion," No. 25, verses 63-76)

Here in summary form are some additional commands found in Sura "The Children of Israel," No. 17.

Show kindness to parents, especially when they are old.

Share your material blessings with relatives, with the poor and with travelers.

Do not waste money.

Take care of orphans.

Use just weights and measures.

These examples suffice to make clear that Islam stresses the same virtues and deplores the same vices that Christianity does. Islam demands of its adherents unselfishness, kindness, justice, endurance, hospitality, purity and honesty.

One particular Qur'anic injunction provides the ethical basis for a strong sense of social responsibility. Sura "The Family of 'Imran," No. 3, verse 104, says, "May you form a nation of those who summon to blessing, who command what is good and forbid what is evil." The expression, "commanding the good and forbidding the evil," became a powerful watchword to help Muslims maintain a healthy moral environment. It is especially applicable to those in roles of authority. The effort of public officials to promote moral behavior is an important part of Islamic political activity.

The Family

The Christian concepts of marriage as a sacrament of the faith or as a concrete image of the union between Christ and the church (Ephesians 5:21-33) have no parallel in Islam. According to the principles of the shari'a, the union of man and woman in marriage is a legal contract. Readers unaccustomed to the functions of religious law should not assume that because Islamic marriage is only a legal contract it is less seriously entered into or is less highly regarded for that reason. On the contrary, the concept of marriage as a divinely ordained law imparts to the union of woman and man a deep religious meaning.

Muslim marriage partners regard their relationship as a shared life of obedience to God in which they enjoy a full range of emotional and spiritual satisfaction. In the Qur'an, Sura "The Romans," No. 30, verse 21, says, "One of the signs of God is

In the Garden

Adam and Eve, from a Persian manuscript of a work by Abu Sa'id Baktishu (died 1058) on "the advantages derived from animals." The Qur'an refers to Adam twenty-five times, mentioning Adam as a creature made from clay, yet one with whom God made a covenant. The garden, the tree and the loss of the garden through disobedience are described in Sura 7, "The Battlements," and other places. Often, "Adam" seems to be used as a collective word for humankind rather than as an individual. The Qur'an mentions Adam's "mate," but the mate is not named. It is not in the Qur'an but in the Hadith literature that Eve (Hawwa') is named and her creation from Adam's rib described. Photo: The Pierpont Morgan Library, New York. M. 500 F. 4v.

this, that He created for you spouses like yourselves, that you might find rest in them, and He put mutual love and mercy in your hearts. This is surely a lesson for thoughtful people." One great purpose of marriage in Islam is to create a couple, each partner being drawn from a previously solitary life, so that they can mutually enrich each other's life and contribute as an entity to the good of society. An ancient Muslim leader is quoted as saying, "A family lacking the spirit of companionship is bereft of divine blessing." The other purpose of marriage is, of course, to produce children and then raise them to be healthy and faithful members of the community. "The Creator of the heavens and the earth has given you partners. . . . That is the way you are multiplied" (Sura "Counsel," No. 42, verse 11).

Because marriage establishes a close link between the families of the spouses, Islamic law and practice stress the importance of consultation with parents by young people who contemplate marriage. However, the law makes completely clear that the main condition for the validity of a marriage is the free consent of both parties. Some criteria for the choice of a mate are faith, morality, financial condition and compatibility. Islamic law outlines in detail the prohibition of marriage for reasons of consanguinity and affinity, and it stipulates the wording of the marriage contract. The wife is assured financial independence from her husband, although in the bonds of marital friendship they are expected to share their resources. The husband is required by the terms of the contract to provide the necessities of life for his wife.

Polygamy is permitted in Islam, with a limit of four wives to one husband. This practice was a means of providing for widows and unmarried women, who in ancient times greatly outnumbered men. The unmarried state was looked upon with disfavor, so the best provision for the times was to allow men to have more than one wife. Islam strictly controls the practice of polygamy, and the Qur'an says that if a husband cannot be equally just to all four wives then he should have only one. For economic and social reasons, polygamy is much less common in the contemporary Islamic world than one might suppose.

Divorce is permitted in Islamic society, although it is called an abominable practice in the sight of God and is allowed only as a concession to human weakness. No custom in Islam has been more reviled by hostile critics than the apparent ease with which a husband can divorce his wife. However, those critics have chosen to overlook the elaborate safeguards that Islamic law provides to protect marriage. For example, the Qur'an directs: "If a husband and wife fear a breach between them let arbiters be appointed from his family and from hers. If they desire reconciliation God will bring about harmony between them" (Sura "The Women," No. 4, verse 35).

Divorce proceedings may be initiated by the woman, by the man, or by the couple, upon mutual agreement to terminate the marriage contract. There are measures to provide for the custody and care of children of divorced parents. On the whole, abuse of the right to divorce does not seem to be any greater in Islamic societies than in non-Muslim ones, including those of North America, in spite of stories told by disparaging observers who visit Muslim lands but know little of the social and cultural environment in which the people live. In fact, sympathetic non-Muslims have remarked at the stability and strength of Muslim families in general.

To conclude this brief discussion and provide a bridge to the next subsection, I shall comment briefly on the notorious right of the Muslim husband to repudiate his wife simply by pronouncing his intention to do so three times. This right is not granted by the Qur'an, but results from the development of rules elaborated by legal scholars. The threefold pronouncement is the third of three types of marital separation, which are graded by specialists in order of legal merit. The type in question here is the least regarded. The very existence of this practice, however, points out a question of great interest to modern observers of Islam: "What is the position of women in that religion?"

The Position of Women

Whatever else may be said about the relationship between the sexes, one thing is sure. The Qur'an and the traditions of the Prophet insist on the equality of woman and man.

> *O humankind, we created you from a male and a*
> *female, and made of you peoples and tribes, in order*
> *that you might learn about each other. Surely the*
> *noblest among you is the one who is most godly.*
> (Sura "The Chambers," No. 49, verse 13)

> *The Prophet said, "All people are equal, as equal as the*
> *teeth of a comb. An Arab is no better than a non-*
> *Arab, nor is a white person over a black person, nor is*
> *the male superior to the female. The only people who*
> *enjoy preference with God are the devout."* (Hadith)

Other points made in the Qur'an, along with some facts of Islamic life, support this clear affirmation of equality between the sexes.

Often in the Qur'an the two sexes are mentioned together explicitly; for example, when speaking of believers, it might say, "male believers" and "female believers" instead of simply using the masculine form to include both sexes.

A women is expected to fulfill the duties of the five pillars

Some Rights and Responsibilities of Women in Islam

WORSHIP: All Muslims are required to know the salat (ritual prayer prayed five times daily) and other devotional duties. When two or more Muslims are together at the time of salat, as are these women outside a mosque in Cairo, one serves as imam ("leader") for the others. Women may thus serve as imam for other women, but not for a mixed congregation of males and females. (United Nations photo, 152,173, by John Isaac.)

INHERITANCE AND OWNERSHIP OF PROPERTY: According to the Qur'an (Sura 4:11), women are entitled to inherit property, although only at the rate of one-half that of men. The recognition of the right of women to inherit was clearly a positive reform over practices in early Arabia. While the picture has been mixed, and many women have been cheated out of their inheritance or simply may not have known how to take advantage of it, it remains true that until recently the ability of a woman to own and manage property in the Islamic system represented a significant advantage for her over her sisters in Europe and the United States.

VEILING AND SECLUSION: The Qur'an itself does not suggest either that women should be veiled or that they should be kept apart from the world of men. On the contrary, the Qur'an is insistent on the full participation of women in society and in the religious practices prescribed for men. It does say (Sura 24:30-31) that the wives of the Prophet were to speak to men from behind a partition for propriety, and that women should not expose themselves immodestly. . . . Some say that the specific verses in the Qur'an relating to separation applied only to the wives of the Prophet, while others assert that they apply to all Muslim women.

(Last two items adapted with permission from "The Experience of Muslim Women," by Jane I. Smith in *The Islamic Impact*, edited by Haddad, Haines and Findly (Syracuse: Syracuse University Press, 1984), pp. 89-112.

just as a man is. In some countries women are discouraged from attending the communal services at the mosque, but this is a local distortion of the universal application of the duties of worship to both sexes. In the Arab Muslim countries of North Africa with which this writer is most familiar, women go to the mosque freely and in great numbers.

After marriage a woman retains the right to independent ownership of her property and can dispose of it as she wishes. She is not obliged to spend it on her family. A woman keeps her maiden name after marriage. This custom is not Islamic in origin and may vary slightly depending on an area's language and culture. However, it continues unchanged in the Arab world and other large population areas of Islam.

A woman has the right to inherit property, but she receives only one-half of the portion that a man inherits. This is explained as a measure commensurate with the woman's advantage in being able to keep her wealth independently of her husband and the husband's extra need for resources to provide for his family, thus making it right for him to inherit more than the woman.

There has never been any legal hindrance to a woman practicing a profession or seeking work outside the home, although Islam gives first priority to a woman's domestic occupations. At various times in Islamic history, women have excelled in many fields of knowledge and expertise. In the very early years some women even fought on the battlefield.

Although Islam arose in a male-dominated culture, its laws promoted a distinct improvement in the condition of women. In fact, Muslims point to pre-Islamic customs such as female infanticide and denial of the right of women to inherit property that were abolished by the law of Islam. They affirm that Islam has been a liberating and enlightening force for women.

At the same time, the strong influence of Islam has not eliminated everywhere the power of male dominance in human relationships. In spite of religious teachings of equality, men in many Muslim cultures have continued to take advantage of women, contrary to the Qur'an. Also many cultural patterns, not Islamic in origin, such as the seclusion of women, moral double standards for men and women, and customs of dress, have been used by men to dominate women. Men have even distorted Islamic religious teaching to justify their discriminatory behavior. Yet in those teachings, as we have seen, are found principles of respect for women's rights. Discrimination against women in

Muslim as well as in Christian societies occurs because of the moral aberrance of members of those societies. Such ethical shortcomings have at times been so serious that strictures against women have even been incorporated into the customs of the people and written into the legal interpretations. Yet it is important for us to understand that Islam as a way of life does not have a bias against women, and also to realize that historically, Muslims have no better or worse a record than Christians in living up to their ideals.

Social Justice and Human Rights

Any discussion of social justice today takes place against the background of the Universal Declaration of Human Rights, proclaimed in 1948 by the General Assembly of the United Nations. Muslims find no difficulty with the content and intent of that document. In fact, they say that from its beginnings Islam has recognized the dignity of human beings and assured the protection of their inalienable rights. In the Qur'an God says, "We have granted honor to the children of Adam" (Sura "The Children of Israel," No. 17, verse 70).

Two remarks are pertinent here, however. Because Islam is so God-centered, it speaks of duties more often than of rights when talking about social justice. When precepts are lived out in faith, there should be no difference between the language of rights and that of duties; if believers fulfill their social duties, then justice will be achieved and the rights of all will be protected. The focus on duties fulfills the theological function of keeping God, rather than human beings, at the center of life. As an example, the U.N. Declaration says that men and women have the *right* to marriage with their free consent. Islam says it is the *duty* under God of all involved—parents, guardians and legal authorities—to procure the free and full consent of the intending spouses.

Also, many Muslims, especially those in predominantly Muslim countries, point out that the U.N. document is less than universal in its wording because it reflects ways of life found in Western, technologically advanced nations. The Declaration, they say, presupposes pluralism, individualism and an outlook on politics and economics that is strange to many societies. If this is the case, then we should not be surprised to find human rights interpreted differently by Western nations and by some peoples of Asia and Africa whose way of life is solidly Islamic.

The right of freedom of religion offers one example of different interpretations. On the one hand, the Qur'an contains a great watchword, "There is no coercion in matters of religion" (Sura "The Cow," No. 2, verse 256), that has vitally affected Islamic policies toward people of other religions throughout history. Forcing conversion to Islam and persecuting non-Muslims were prohibited from the beginning. And today, Muslim governments are careful to protect minorities' rights to practice a religion other than that of the majority. However, when members of a homogeneous Muslim society think of religious freedom they do not think primarily of the right of individuals to choose or change their religion. Their main concern is the right of the people to practice Islam freely, unhindered by such alien ideologies as atheism and materialism, by political tyrants, or by subversive agents who might try to undermine the peoples'

When Justice Rules

The great Persian poet, Sa'di (died ca. 1290) delighted in storytelling, wit and wisdom. He also wrote fine prose, and his courageous words to the great often come as a heartening surprise. In this tale in prose and verse he points to a moral of political significance. The hero is conventionally one of the heroic Persian rulers from the "good old days" when justice ruled the land.

They tell how, when some game was being roasted for Nushirvan the Just during a hunting expedition, no salt was available. So an attendant was sent to a village to get some. Nushirvan said, 'Pay for the salt, lest the village be ruined and a bad precedent be established.'

When asked what harm could come from such a small amount, Nushirvan replied: 'The first foundation of oppression in the world was little, but those who came after added to it so that it reached its present culmination.'

If the king eats one apple from the garden of a subject,
　His attendants will dig up the tree by the roots.
For every half-egg the sultan allows to be taken unjustly
　His troops will put a thousand fowls upon the spit.

A tyrant of ill fortune will not endure,
　But the curse on him abides for ever.

Tale and information from "Persian Literature: An Affirmation of Identity," by G. M. Wickens in *Introduction to Islamic Civilisation*, edited by R.M. Savory (Cambridge: Cambridge University Press, 1976), page 74. Used by permission.

confidence in and loyalty to their faith tradition. Measures taken to protect the rights to religious liberty understood in this way, however, may constitute a suppression of the rights of others who might want to propagate their non-Muslim beliefs in a solidly Muslim society. This is one reason why Christian missionary work in Muslim lands is problematical.

Selecting a few topics from the wide range dealt with by Muslims in seeking social justice, I shall briefly describe some issues of politics, including war and peace; crime and punishment; and economics. These subjects include most of the articles of the Universal Declaration of Human Rights.

Politics

The Islamic view of government is that God is sovereign over all human affairs, including those activities concerning the political grouping of people called a state or a nation. No human group, then, can rightfully claim to be fully independent or autonomous. The concept that God is the real ruler has led some people to describe the Islamic political model as a theocracy, or a rule by God. But Muslims do not accept this description. In their view, a theocracy requires a specially designated ruling class, priestly or other, to carry out the divine rule. And Islam has no priesthood.

Along with the concept of God's overall authority, Muslims believe in prophethood. God, the sovereign, makes known the laws that are needful for any people, at any time, through the intermediary of prophets. The Prophet Muhammad brought the law, the shari'a, as contained in the Qur'an and the hadith, to provide the basis for Islamic political life. It is important to realize that this law is considered to be of divine origin. It is God's revealed law and is therefore adequate and necessary for human government.

A third principle in addition to God's ultimate authority and the reality of prophethood as the basis for Islamic politics is *khilafa*, roughly translated, "deputyship." From khilafa derives "caliph," the name given to the human authority in the former Muslim empire. Theoretically, the office of khilafa or deputyship is open to the whole community of Muslims. God has designated the entire people to administer their own affairs according to the terms of divine law. This is not popular sovereignty in the Western, democratic tradition. In a democratic state the people *make* their own laws. In Islam the "deputies," who are the believers, are required to *carry out* the shari'a. The means to do so is broadly called "consultation," or *shura*. When consultation among all concerned citizens is practiced, a real democratic spirit presides over the work of governing an Islamic state. In the Qur'an, God directs Muhammad to consult his people about the conduct of their affairs, and, once a decision is made, to "trust in God" (Sura "The Family of 'Imran", No. 3, verse 159).

According to these political principles, the way is open for any of several types of political organization. Islam does not advocate a particular form of government such as a republic or a monarchy. One decision the community has to make is who will be their leader, under God. The main thing is that the one chosen to govern is righteous, knowledgeable about Islam and able to administer justice. Rulers are accountable to all Muslims for their actions.

It is clear that in order to carry out these political principles, Muslims must be in control of their own affairs in their own territory. This is precisely what has *not* been the case during much of the twentieth century. But now, with Muslim countries being politically free of outside control, there is intense activity and discussion in those lands about how the citizens should carry out their desire to have Islamic government.

Millions of Muslims live in countries where they are a minority of the population. For them there is little hope of implementing their political doctrine. Some may hope that in the future an Islamic state will become possible, but as a rule, minority Muslims in countries such as Canada, the USA and West Germany are just beginning to reflect seriously on how or whether their political ideals can be adapted to pluralistic societies in which they are but few voices among many.

Many Christians wonder about the ways in which religious minorities were and are treated in Islamic countries. The law of Islam provides a place within the social structure for those groups, even though the vast majority of the population might be Muslim. Formerly, this status for minorities was called *dhimmi*, or protected citizens. The dhimmi people were mostly Christians and Jews, who, in return for the freedom to practice their religion and be governed to a degree by their own religious law, paid a special tax called the *jizya* to the Muslim government. The rights and privileges of dhimmi people were different from those of the majority. Even though the dhimmi status is considered today to be undesirable by members of minority groups, it is helpful to know that for many centuries these ancient laws protected Christians and Jews from the grosser forms of religious discrimination and persecution that were common outside the domains of Islam.

Today a pressing question in interfaith relations is how Christian, Jewish and other religious minorities are to be treated under Islamic governments. These governments are confident that if they are left alone by outside powers and permitted to implement Islamic law in its fullness, minorities will be given justice and freedom. Members of the religious minorities are less confident of this, however, and have no desire to return to the status of dhimmi.

Another aspect of politics concerns war and peace. Islam sees itself as the key to peace in the world, whether for individuals or for nations. The shari'a, if followed, provides a balance between individual and collective interests, so that there need be no insoluble conflict between individuals or between groups. In the Muslim view, all peoples, unfortunately, have not submitted to God's rule, so the threat of aggression against the Islamic community is real. War is permitted to protect the interests of Islam. Muslims are obliged to take part in such a war when it proves necessary. This defensive warfare, the "just war" of Islam, is called *jihad*, a term much used today amid turbulent events on the world scene. The meaning of jihad is distorted when it is translated "holy war." And some Muslim groups do abuse its legal meaning by making it a slogan for their aggressive military and even terrorist actions. Properly conceived, jihad is a religious duty like all political duties. And the righteous practice of jihad is safeguarded by an abundance of rules applying to all aspects of its conduct. Muslims have pointed out, too, that jihad has a meaning broader than "just war": it involves a believer's earnest moral effort to carry out the precepts of Islam. It means "an extraordinary effort to do one's duty in the path of God."

Crime and Punishment

Because Muslim practice of punishing certain crimes with great severity has been much critized by outsiders, it will help us to know how Muslims understand this part of their system. At first it may strike us as unusual that crime and punishment form part of religious law. Most Christians today are accustomed to considering these matters as functions of civil or secular law, although we recognize that they were dealt with by the ancient Hebrew religion as described in the Old Testament. The rules on crime and punishment fit into the vast and integrated whole of Islamic life. Criminal law is not the only, nor even the main, factor to deter and prevent crime in a Muslim society. There is the believers' faith, making them desire to follow and please God by obeying the positive moral principles we have described. There is the collective ethical responsibility, also described above, whereby all men and women take it upon themselves to exhort one another to do good and to avoid evil. Thus an environment of sensitivity to righteous behavior is the setting for laws on crime and punishment.

Next, Islam considers that the consequences of a crime are finally removed by God only when the guilty person repents and seeks forgiveness. Legal punishments do not serve to atone for the crime. Rather, they represent the need of the society to protect and strengthen itself against violent acts by its members.

Because the subject of penal law is not fully treated in the Qur'an, its details have had to be worked out by legal specialists, basing rules on principles, and, in some cases, on specific prescriptions contained in the Qur'an and the hadith. Capital punishment is prescribed for those who forsake Islam, called apostates; for those who commit intentional murder; and for those who commit adultery. The rule regarding apostates has now become obsolete. Not all legal interpreters agree that adulterers should pay with their lives.

Flogging is the penalty for fornication, sometimes for adultery, and, according to many authorities, for drinking alcohol. In addition, one who falsely accuses another of adultery is liable to flogging.

The punishment for theft is the cutting off of the hand. Those guilty of armed robbery are also liable to the same punishment, or, if they kill their victims, they are to be executed.

All of these severe punishments are surrounded with complex conditions that limit the extent to which they are carried out. Punishment is less severe, or is even waived, in such circumstances as confession by the guilty, lack of proof of guilt, or agreement on payment of damages to the wronged party. For a whole range of offenses against public morals and good order, or in violation of individuals' rights, punishment is left to the discretion of the judge.

The application of the Islamic penal code is not consistent in various parts of the world. Many countries possess, as a legacy from their colonial masters of the last century, legal systems that are foreign to Islam but are adapted to such circumstances of modern life as international commerce and labor relations. Muslim peoples have not achieved universal agreement on how the ancient code should be applied in regard to such modern affronts to human dignity as drug dealing and terrorism.

Economics

Some readers may be surprised to know that Muslims hold to a specific doctrine that they call Islamic economics. In a world accustomed to the hard-nosed materialism of economic realities in a secular environment, it sounds excessively idealistic to speak of economics as linked with morals and religious truth. But this is precisely what Muslims do, and they find a moral doctrine of economics perfectly consistent with their overall view of the world as created and sustained by Almighty God. Even as the Islamic political doctrine begins with the absolute rulership of God, so the Islamic economic doctrine begins with the absolute ownership of all things by God. Human beings can own property; in fact, Islam encourages private ownership, as long as owners confess that they are only stewards of the Great Owner who is God.

The headquarters of the Islamic Development Bank (IDB) in Jiddah, Saudi Arabia, and its president, Dr. Ahmad Mohamed Ali (at left). Founded in 1975, the IDB has 45 member countries. It provides short- and long-term financing of development and trade projects as well as technical assistance. Illustration by Norman Macdonald, article by Rami G. Khouri, courtesy *Aramco World*, May-June 1987.

The human drive to satisfy earthly needs by the production of goods and by commerce is fully supported by Muslim teaching. No stigma is attached to accumulating wealth, provided that in doing so the person engages in honorable, lawful activities. However, this forthright acceptance of individual economic activity for self-interest is balanced by the teaching on social responsibility. The owner of wealth is in partnership with the community to achieve a balanced, harmonious economic life. Another great Qur'anic watchword is applied here. God says to the Muslims, "We have made you a people of 'the middle way,' so that you might be witnesses to humankind" (Sura "The Cow," No. 2, verse 143). The expression, "people of the middle way," has been variously interpreted, but often it is used to contrast Muslim economics with what are termed the "extreme ways" of capitalism and communism. According to this view, capitalism encourages unbridled individualism and uncontrolled concentration of wealth in a few selfish hands. Communism is seen as rigid collectivism, where the individual counts for nothing, and only the interests of the state are served. By contrast, Islam, "the middle way," balances individual and collective interests. It also furnishes the impetus for economic activity that furthers both the material goal of improving the condition of the people and the spiritual goal of seeking God's pleasure. This latter exalted motive for accumulating material goods should prevent Muslims from falling into the snare of materialism.

The teachings of the religion, ever adapted to human need, provide three great controls, or checks, on the greed and selfishness of those who engage in the struggle for economic gain.

The first is the duty of *zakat*, which we have already considered. I translated zakat as "contribution to charity," but because of the patronizing way in which the word "charity" has been used in modern times, many Muslims prefer to avoid using it to translate zakat. They see the duty as a social tax, intended to provide at all times for the extraordinary needs of the poverty-stricken and the unfortunate. "Tax," however, can connote economic necessity and governmental intrusion into private life, which zakat is not. It is an act of worship, obligatory of course, but expressing the religious and moral implications that underlie all economic activity. In the view of many, zakat is the forerunner of modern social security and welfare laws. And for individual Muslims who pay zakat, the duty is a permanent reminder that one great reason for earning wealth is to share it

---

Some Banking Techniques

Some of the basic financial techniques of Islamic banking, known by their Arabic names, which involve forms of participation that Western banks do not undertake:

Mudaraba: An Islamic bank lends money to a client—to finance a factory, for example—in return for which the banks will get a specified percentage of the factory's net profits every year for a designated period. The share of the profits provides for repayment of the principal and a profit for the bank to pass on to its depositors. Should the factory lose money, the bank, its depostiors and the borrower all jointly absorb the losses, thereby putting into practice the pivotal Islamic principal that the providers and users of capital should share risks and rewards.

Muqarada: This novel technique allows a bank to float what are effectively Islamic bonds to finance a specific project. Investors who buy *muqaradah* bonds take a share of the profits of the project being financed, but also share the risk of unexpectedly low profits, or even losses. They have no say in the management of the project, but act as non-voting shareholders.

Ijara-ijara wa iktina: Equivalent to the leasing and installment loan, or hire-purchase, practices that put millions of drivers on the road each year, these techniques as applied by Islamic banks include the requirement that the leased items be used productively and in ways permitted by Islamic law.

Adapted from "Islamic Banking: Knotting a New Network," by Rami G. Khouri, courtesy of *Aramco World*, May-June 1987.

---

with the less fortunate. The Qur'an warns: "Those who are stingy with the bounty that God has bestowed upon them should not think that they are better off. No, they are worse off. That with which they are stingy will be hung around their necks on the Day of Resurrection" (Sura "The Family of 'Imran," No. 3, verse 180).

The second check on human greed is the prohibition of usury—payment of interest on loans. Usury is considered the opposite of zakat, since it is a selfish taking advantage of the borrower. But to prohibit paying interest, or *riba*, as it is called in the Qur'an, contradicts the whole banking system developed in Europe and North America. A faithful Muslim is forbidden to collect interest even on savings deposits. The Qur'an says, "O believers, obey God and give up any usury that might remain to you, if you are truly believers" (Sura "The Cow," No. 2, verse 278). So it is difficult for Muslims to obey their economic doctrine while they live in Western nations.

The prohibition of riba is based on the belief that money is only a medium of exchange, that it has no value in itself, so it should not be used to make more money. This does not mean that Islam is against investment, but by prohibiting interest the doctrine requires that investors share the risks involved in the enterprises that are being promoted by their money. If money is invested through a bank, then the depositor (as investor), the bank and the borrower should all share in the risks of the project being financed, either taking losses together or receiving profits together. Muslims consider this method of investing to be not only in keeping with the nature of money but also to be a humane, fair and equitable way of conducting business. They point out that in Western banking the borrower must assume the major burden, because the interest paid to the bank and that paid by the bank to the depositor are guaranteed. Only the borrower is subject to the risks of success or failure in the enterprise.

In Islamic countries as well as in other places in the world, a considerable movement is growing to establish banks, both national and international, that practice the Muslim doctrine of investment.

Some Muslims claim that the intent of the Qur'an in prohibiting riba is to stop lenders from charging excessive rates of interest. These persons feel that they can participate in Western banking and still remain faithful to their religion, since secular anti-usury laws control the amount of interest that can be charged. However, a great many others hold to the absolute prohibition of riba as a divinely ordered curb on human greed.

Finally, the Islamic laws of inheritance, when followed faithfully, help prevent the hoarding of wealth by a few. This is a complex subject, but in general, owners of property are prohibited by Islamic law from bequeathing more than one-third of their possessions to persons of their choice. The other two-thirds of the estate, or all of it if there is no will, is distributed to members of the family according to careful rules that provide a fair share for all persons involved. Such a division of the estate effectively prevents individuals from amassing large fortunes by inheritance alone.

4

Great Themes of Islamic Life

*I*n Chapter 3 we considered Islamic practices and attitudes; now we shall look at how certain ideas or themes function to mark the peoples of Islam as distinctive. I have chosen four themes that I believe represent very influential factors in Muslim religious life.

Peoplehood: The Umma

No matter how well educated or how uninstructed Muslims may be in the sciences of Islam, no matter how modern or how old-fashioned they might feel themselves to be, no matter how fervent or indifferent in formal religious practice, all resonate to the theme of the *umma*. This word found in the Qur'an can be translated as "people" or "community" or "nation."

A Definition of the Umma

Islam brought peoples from all tribes, nations, ethnic groups and races into a new grouping, based only on faith in the one living God. This grouping was called the *umma* of Islam. The Qur'an speaks to Muslims in inspiring tones, saying: "You are the best community (umma) that has been raised up for humankind" (Sura "The Family of 'Imran," No. 3, verse 110). The force of this new entity in religious history was proved during the first centuries of Islam when peoples of all cultures and languages became part of the umma. A partial list of peoples who united religiously under the inspiration of Islam includes the Spanish, Slavs, Berbers, Syrians, Turks, Chinese, Phoenicians, Copts, Ethiopians, Persians, Indians, East Indians and Sudanese, in addition to the Arabs. During the first century of Islam, conflict arose between Arab and non-Arab elements in the community, but as the religion grew, racial and ethnic distinctions lost their importance. One of the most admirable features of the Islamic system is its relative freedom from racial prejudice.

The umma idea has concrete implications for the future. Its all-encompassing blueprint for society is intended to provide a harmonious and fruitful environment for the whole world. Because no more prophets will come after Muhammad, according to the doctrine of prophethood, and because Islam is the "best" umma, Muslims believe that it is only a matter of time before the whole world will recognize that its best choice is Islam. At the same time, there is no way in which Muslims should try to force their religion upon the rest of the world. They are conscious of the dictum mentioned earlier: "There is no coercion in matters of religion." They tolerate other religious communities, although they believe that finally all religions except Islam will disappear.

The Nature of Islam's Unity

Some readers may think that I have overstated the unity of Islam, in view of the disunited image that the Muslim world presently projects. Questions of diversity and disunity will be treated a little later. But before differences can be understood, we must appreciate the nature of Islamic unity. It is this common approach to religion on a worldwide scale that makes it possible even to talk about something called "Islam." Most of the uniting factors have already been described. It remains simply to underscore the simple and direct ways in which they succeed in binding together the bewildering diversity of the Islamic peoples into a unity of practice. It should be noted again that Islamic unity is very practical. Islam holds no *doctrine* of unity, or *mystery* of unity. The practice of the umma simply serves to cement the worldwide community together.

The practice of salat, or ritual prayer, is a uniting rite. Whether Muslims find themselves in Damascus or in Tokyo, in San Francisco or in Nairobi, they fit in easily with the way prayer is performed. Variations in the gestures and words are so slight as to be inconsequential.

The unifying capacity of Islamic prayer is enhanced by the use of a single liturgical language. Prayers are universally recited in Arabic. The meanings of the Qur'an may be explained in Hausa, in Chinese or in French, for example, but when worshipers pray "The Opener" (Sura 1 of the Qur'an) they all do so in Arabic.

Also recited in the salat is the creed, or shahada, described earlier. This two-part statement of faith, so clear-cut and unambiguous, is another feature that unites all Muslims.

The multicultural mosque in Panfilov, in the Kazakstan SSR a few miles west of the USSR border with China. The area west of Panfilov was conquered in the eighth century A.D. by the great Arab general Qutaiba Ibn Muslim. In the tenth century, the ruler of Kashgar became a Muslim, and the people of western China have remained Muslim. The mosque's facade is typical of the austere Islamic architecture of Central Asia, while the minaret is shaped like an ornate Chinese pagoda. Photo by Tor Eigeland, courtesy of *Aramco World*, July-August 1988.

Even geography takes on a unifying focus in Islam—the qibla, or direction of Mecca, toward which worshipers face when they pray. The niche in the mosque wall marks this physical orientation for the multitudes of Islam, wherever they may find themselves (see page 37). And, of course, the pilgrimage to Mecca, as has already been noted, is Islam's culminating, spectacular expression of unity.

One other element, perhaps the most subtle and pervading, is the example of the Prophet Muhammad. That example of behavior and attitude, known as the *sunna* of the Prophet, was observed, reported and recorded by early Muslims. The books of hadith contain a record of the sunna. The normative example of Muhammad is revered everywhere and affects literally everything that Muslims do, from intimate details of personal hygiene to ways of doing business. In many respects the centrality of the Prophet in Islamic life justifies the often-heard expression that the umma is the umma of the Prophet.

Diversity Within the Umma

Now that we have some idea of the ties that bind Islamic peoples together, we can better consider elements of diversity within the worldwide community. Islam allows room for divergence of opinion. The Prophet Muhammad is quoted as saying, "Differences in my community are a mercy." The capacity to accommodate different opinions and tendencies and even to find in them a source of enrichment is one of the strengths of Islam. It may stem from the *absence* of a doctrine of the unity of the umma. That unity simply flows out of the doctrine of God's oneness. Even as the world created by the one God is of indescribable variety, so the community issuing from faith in that God is of remarkable complexity in its composition and its points of view.

Historically, Islam has never broken into denominations as has the Christian world. Whatever serious divisions have marked Islamic history have not crystallized into institutional structures, very possibly because Islam has no structure corresponding to the church. The notion of umma may suggest to Christians the idea of "church" in its universal sense, but Muslims did not develop either a local or a centralized religious organization that distinguishes itself from other institutions of society. The umma, whether local or transnational, carries with it the strong sense of peoplehood rather than a sense of being "called out" from the rest of society to "belong" to an institution called "umma"

Schools of Islamic Law

The development of various schools of law helped preserve the diversity of Islamic law which was sanctioned by the reported saying of the Prophet, "Difference of opinion within my community is a sign of the bounty of Allah." These schools took their names from their founders. Although there had been many law schools by A.D. 1300, four major Sunni schools predominated. Today they predominate in the following areas: The Hanafi in the Middle East and the Indian subcontinent, the Maliki in North, Central and West Africa, the Shafii in East Africa and southeast Asia, and the Hanbali in Saudi Arabia.

In addition to Sunni law schools, there are Shi'a schools such as the Jafari in Iran and Iraq.

Quoted by permission from "Law in Islam" by John L. Esposito in *The Islamic Impact*, edited by Haddad, Haines and Findly (Syracuse: Syracuse University Press, 1984), page 75.

---

or "Islam." People of the umma permeate all institutions of society, thus making it possible to speak of an Islamic society. Of course, now that Islam is exerting such a strong influence in countries where religious pluralism is the norm, Muslims in the future may feel obliged to adopt a more "institutional" approach to protect and make known their identity as a people.

Until now, the story of divergence in the umma has been one of continual ferment. Various parties have striven for influence: sometimes they have quarrelled and fought. The details of these debates are too complex for our present purpose. We simply note that Muslims have differed over political, social, ethical, economic, legal, philosophical and theological matters as well as over types of spirituality. Signs of ancient debates may be seen today, for example, in the four schools of Islamic law, and in scattered pockets of descendants from sectarian movements of long ago. For our purposes we need to consider three groups from the past, because they constitute vital forces of present-day Islam. Later we shall take a brief look at the geographical and cultural scope of the umma, with emphasis on the Islamic presence in North America.

The Sunnis

These Muslims represent perhaps ninety percent of the world-wide community of Islam. They call themselves the People of the Sunna, that is, those who respect and follow the normative example of the Prophet Muhammad. *Sunni* is the singular form of the noun derived from *sunna* and, as a convenience when speaking in English, most people add an "s" to form the plural. Attempts to categorize Sunnis further by calling them the "orthodox" Muslims are not correct, because Islam has no central authority to define an "orthodox" position. As we have seen, Muslims in general agree on matters of belief and law, but Sunnis have a very egalitarian system with a multitude of authorities and points of view, all held together by their allegiance to the sunna of the Prophet. In fact it would serve little purpose to differentiate this vast group by the term Sunnis if it were not for the need to distinguish them from the remaining ten percent who form the second group.

The Shi'a

The most important theological and political controversy among Muslims began during the first centuries of the Islamic era, leading to division of the community. Today we can see the results of that great division in the country of Iran and, to a lesser degree, in some other Middle Eastern lands. In the seventh and eighth centuries A.D., a party of Muslims emerged who felt that the leadership of the community belonged rightly in the hands of a member of the Prophet's family. The rest of the Muslims, who later were distinguished by the name of Sunnis, believed that any properly qualified and universally respected Muslim could be a leader. After the death of the Prophet Muhammad, the first few leaders of the umma were chosen by a consensus of the people. Sunnis concluded from this historical fact that Muhammad did not name a successor. However, the *Shi'a*, or partisans of the Prophet's Household, maintained that Muhammad really did prefer his cousin and son-in-law, 'Ali, and that this preference was suppressed by leaders who had another opinion on the succession. When 'Ali was finally chosen as the third caliph, his partisans thought they had achieved victory for their leader. However, 'Ali only governed from 656 to 661 before coming to a violent end.

The next years proved tragic and violent for the partisans of 'Ali as they pursued their policy of promoting the interests of Muhammad's family. The term *Shi'a* gradually came to be applied as a proper name, although its primary meaning is simply "partisans" or "followers." The sign " ' " stands for a sound unknown in English. To designate the singular form of Shi'a, writers resort to several devices, since the Arabic singular is difficult for English speakers to pronounce. In this book we call a single member of the Shi'a group a Shi'ite, pronounced shē'-ĭt. The system of the Shi'a is called Shi'ism (shē'ĭzm).

Over the centuries the tumultuous history of Shi'ism has involved momentous struggles, rich spiritual and philosophical
development and division into a number of branches. These
branches spread into many parts of the world, becoming concentrated in Iran, Yemen, Iraq and Lebanon.

In view of the present importance of Shi'a on the world scene,
it is important to have some idea of what makes the Shi'a
distinctive. The popular media tend to overplay this distinctiveness, and ill-informed journalists have produced some utterly
unfounded reports concerning the supposed stark contrast
between Sunnis and Shi'a. Before pointing out elements of
originality in Shi'ism, I want to insist on the basic agreement
between the two groups in matters of doctrine and practice. All
we have learned about Islamic patterns of life applies to both
Shi'a and Sunnis, except for questions regarding the leadership
of the Islamic community. Here are the main points of Shi'ite
belief that diverge from the majority point of view.

1. Even as God sent a prophet in the person of Muhammad,
so He appoints representatives of the Prophet, called Imams, to
continue the Prophet's work: guiding the people and upholding
justice. These individuals are believed to be infallible. The Shi'ite
Imams should not be confused with the *imams*, known throughout the Muslim world as the individuals who lead communal
prayers. According to the Shi'a of Iran, there have been twelve
Imams, the last of whom was born in the year 870. He went into
concealment when he was only eight years old and is expected
to return in the future as the restorer of faith and justice to the

---

Shi'te Passion Play

Shi'ites celebrate the first ten days of the first month of the Islamic
liturgical year by commemorating the martyrdom of Husayn, the
son of 'Ali. This observance is marked by communal lamentation
as Shi'ite believers reinact the tragic events that took place on
the battlefield of Karbala in 680 A.D. As a part of the ceremonies
in some places men express the intensity of their mourning by
flagellating themselves. (These scenes are sometimes shown by
Western news media with little explanation of their religious
significance.) The dramatic performances together with processions
and audience participation might best be characterized as a kind
of passion play involving much of the community in any given
locality. Scholars of the Shi'ite leadership have disapproved of these
observances with more or less regularity, saying that they go
contrary to the spirit of Islam. *RMS*

world. Other Shi'a groups hold different views regarding the individual Imams. Until the now-concealed Imam reappears, he is represented by the legal specialists and scholars who are his intermediaries in the community. In Iran these figures are called Ayatollahs.

2. An important part of the Imam's task was to interpret the Qur'an in its spiritual, inner meaning, as well as in its outer, literal meaning. Shi'ism has produced a large number of esoteric philosophers who seek to follow the Imams by interpreting the hidden wisdom of God.

When joined with the events of their history, these distinctive beliefs have caused the Shi'a to develop an outlook that differs from that of the Sunnis. It is difficult to define this outlook further without studying the two systems in depth. But it is safe to say that the elements of unity, described earlier in this chapter, hold Sunnis and Shi'a together more strongly than their divergences keep them apart. In spite of antagonistic attitudes that have marked the history of the two groups, a strong movement is in progress today by representatives of both sides to minimize the divisiveness of the past and to bring these two dimensions of Islam closer together in actual life.

The Sufis

Sufis are the mystics of Islam, so named perhaps because of the wool garment *(suf)* that early ascetics wore. These mystics are found throughout the Muslim community, and can scarcely be called a division of Islam, or even an offshoot. They belong very much to the whole body of the faithful, practicing their mysti-

---

The Sufi Path

The mystical path, as developed and experienced by the early Sufis, is a series of deaths. The motto was "die before ye die!" One has first to die to one's lowly qualities and replace them by positive qualities. The idea of sacrificing part of one's lower self every day, of dying to one's self and being revived on a higher spiritual level, permeated Sufism in all its shades. The secret of being reborn has been expressed by the Sufis in numerous symbols and metaphors, such as, among many others, the moth casting itself into the flame of the candle, or the rain drop that sinks into the depths of the ocean ... [or, in later Sufi poetry, images of] longing to die for the sake of the Divine Beloved or ... [on] the battlefield of love.
Quoted by permission from "Aspects of Mystical Thought in Islam," by Annemarie Schimmel in *The Islamic Impact*, edited by Haddad, Haines and Findly (Syracuse: Syracuse University Press, 1984), pages 116-117.

cism in addition to the normal, universal observances of the religion and whatever other occupations they may have in life. Many of the greatest Islamic religious scholars and legal specialists have also been Sufis. Mystical doctrines have inspired some of the supreme masterpieces of Islamic literature. At the same time, laypeople have access to Sufi activity by becoming members of the orders that have arisen around the figures and teachings of famous personalities.

The history of Sufism is an awe-inspiring record of spiritual aspiration and achievement. The movement began with ascetics who went beyond the balanced, world-accepting spirituality of the normal Muslim experience. Along with the severe discipline of rough clothing, fasting, vigils, withdrawal from human company and silence, the mystics stressed patience, trust in God, fear of God, purification of the soul, and love. They elaborated litanies and formulas of self-examination, of praise to God and of communal spiritual enthusiasm that sometimes brought the practitioners into trances of ecstasy.

As the movement progressed, Sufi thinkers began to see their spiritual discipline as a way to ultimate enlightenment, a key to the secret of the universe. To attain this height, though, it was deemed necessary to die to self and live entirely to God. The Sufi philosophers spoke of union with God. Some of their daring teachings offended the more traditional majority of Muslims and by religious consensus, Sufism was never accepted generally. But the Sufi orders, with their efficient organization and coherent practices, accessible to the masses, were and are extremely popular. Nowadays Muslims with a modern, technological

---

A Sufi Tale

Ibrahim ibn Adham (d. 777 A. D.) was one of the early Sufis. According to legend he was the ruler of the Persian city of Balkh at the time of his conversion.

One night, he heard a strange sound on the roof of his palace in Balkh. The servants found a man who claimed, in Ibrahim's presence, to be looking for his lost camel on the palace roof. Blamed by the prince for having undertaken such an impossible task, the man answered that his, Ibrahim's, attempt at attaining heavenly peace and true religious life in the midst of luxury was as absurd as the search for a camel on top of a roof. Ibrahim repented and repudiated all his possessions.

Quoted from the *Mathnawi* of Jalaluddin Rumi, *Mystical Dimensions in Islam*, by Annemarie Schimmel. © 1975, The University of North Carolina Press. Reprinted by permission.

Muslims in the Americas: The Caribbean
Nearly 400,000 Muslims, mostly East Indian in origin, live on at least a dozen Caribbean islands, including Barbados, Grenada, Dominica, Puerto Rico, the U.S. Virgin Islands and Jamaica. The region's heaviest concentrations of Muslims are in Suriname (with an estimated 100,000 believers) and Guyana (with an estimated 120,000), both on the northeast coast of South America, and on the islands of Trinidad and Tobago, home to about 100,000 Muslims.

The oil-rich island of Trinidad boasts the Western hemisphere's highest concentration of mosques—85 in all. Some political leaders here, including the speaker of the house and the president, are Muslims. The photo shows Trinidad's Jinnah Memorial Mosque.

Trinidad's first Muslims were black slaves from the Mandingo tribe of West Africa, many of whose members embraced Islam in the 1740s. Slaves were brought to work Trinidad's sugar plantations

outlook tend to discredit Sufism as being excessively oriented toward the inner life and susceptible to superstition.

Geographical and Cultural Diversity

Continuing the theme of the umma and its diversity, I want to describe a few aspects of the extent of Islam that may not be well-known. The worldwide extension of Islam today reflects centuries of effort by commercial people, teachers and other professionals who moved out across the earth to spread their faith by word and example. Until this generation, Muslims did not have organized missionary agencies with strategies for bringing non-Muslims to Islam. The community grew because of the influence of those Muslims who chose to live and work with people outside the lands of Muslim majority. Beyond the Arab world, Islam's heartland, so to speak, the ancient, powerful civilizations of India, China and the East Indies early experienced the dynamic appeal of faith in Islam, so that today vast numbers of Muslims live side by side with Hindus, Buddhists,

around 1777. Most black slaves had no continuing contact with their homeland and could not sustain their Islamic faith. In recent years, a number of people from African backgrounds have accepted Islam in Trinidad.

Most Trinidadian Muslims trace their ancestry to the Indian state of Uttar Pradesh. When the British abolished slavery in their colonies in 1834, they turned to the system of indentured servitude, which required immigrants to work a number of years to pay off the debts of the often inflated cost of their passage. Indians were brought to Trinidad in the 1840s to work in the sugar plantations. Few of their descendants have any idea about their heritage in India, although many have maintained their Muslim faith.

"The Muslim community in Trinidad, despite being small, is very organized," said businessman Imtiaz Ali. Ali manages the Muslim Credit Union Co-operative Society in Curepe. In keeping with the laws of Islam, the credit union charges the equivalent of $1 a month in dues, while offering its 1,500 members interest-free loans.

Ali describes two generations of Muslims in Trinidad: one that has become set in tradtion, doing things because they were born into it. "This group of people doesn't find Islam very dynamic," said Ali, who is 32. "And then you have a younger generation of Muslims who do." In 1986, he said, nearly 100 Trinidadian Muslims—many from this younger generation—made the Hajj.

Adapted from "Muslims in the Caribbean" by Larry Luxner in *Aramco World*, November-December 1987. Photo by Larry Luxner.

adherents of Chinese religions, Communists, humanists and animists. Even Korea and Japan count sizable Muslim communities. (See chart on page 89.)

North Americans have heard much about the plight of Christians and Jews in the Soviet Union, but not much information has reached us about the fifty million Muslims of Turkic origin who inhabit that vast nation. They too have suffered immeasurably at the hands of a government that is by principle atheistic and anti-religious. However, the Soviet Muslims remain a vital growing religious force, second only to Christians in number.

Although the Balkan states of Europe have had an indigenous population belonging to the Islamic religion since the time of the Turkish Empire, western European countries have experienced a massive influx of Muslims only since the Second World War. Today nearly one million Muslims live in the United Kingdom; Pakistani immigrants are the most influential element. With two million, mostly of North African origin, France has more Muslims than Protestants. And Germany, with about 1.8 million Muslims, is not far behind—by far the largest number of these are immigrants from Turkey.

On the North American continent the number of Muslims is difficult to determine, since religious affiliation is not requested on U.S. and Canadian census forms, and there is no centralized Islamic agency that publishes population figures. A conservative estimate puts the number of Muslims in Canada at 250,000 and in the U.S. at about three million. Islam has become the third largest religion on the continent, and it is growing fast.

The significant presence of Muslim groups in the United States and Canada goes back no more than a century. Historians recount some stories of isolated cases of Muslims who either came to the New World with the Spanish conquistadores or who were brought by slave traders. The first immigrants to constitute communities of Muslims came from Lebanon, Syria, Palestine and Jordan. They came seeking economic opportunities and settled in the Midwest and the Northeast of the U.S. and in the larger cities of Canada. Gradually, others arrived from Arab countries and from the Balkan lands of Europe, then a part of the Ottoman Empire. At first, few Asians came because the laws of the United States and Canada severely restricted the number of Asians permitted to make their home here. Finally, in the post World War II era, immigration policies were liberalized, and a large number of people came to these shores from Muslim lands in the Middle East, the Far East and Africa. Some sought refuge from political upheavals in their homelands. Others came initially to seek higher education and chose to remain. In general, there has been no large-scale immigration of Muslim unskilled laborers. Instead, the newcomers have tended to be professionals and business people. The student population is quite important, although it is constantly changing. By some estimates, Muslims from as many as sixty nations are living in North America. This religious presence in our midst may be considered in three categories: immigrants; students; and indigenous American Muslims.

1. Immigrants sometimes group together according to national origin. Most large cities and some smaller towns, especially in the northern and west-coast areas of the U.S., are home to immigrant communities. The Quincy, Massachusetts, Islamic Center was begun by Lebanese, but today it attracts many nationalities. A vital community life based on Islam and national origin is maintained by the Albanian colony of Waterbury,

Connecticut. In Hartford, Connecticut, Pakistanis and Indians predominate in the Muslim place of worship. In Paterson, New Jersey, lives a Turkish community. In Chicago, believers of Balkan background are prominent. The Detroit, Michigan, and Toledo, Ohio, areas have sizable concentrations of Arabs. Those of Shi'ite persuasion have established a few centers, in Detroit, New York City and other cities, but the divisions between Shi'a and Sunnis are not generally very marked. In Canada, Toronto and Montreal count many vital ethnic groups of Muslims. Near Edmonton, Alberta, Lebanese immigrants keep their Druze community traditions (the Druze faith is related to the Shi'a tradition). According to recent research by Dr. Yvonne Haddad of the University of Massachusetts, over three hundred mosques and centers for immigrant Muslims have been established in the United States. Islamic Centers range from single rented rooms to elaborate structures like the imposing center on Massachusetts Avenue in Washington, D.C. In New Jersey, Muslims have begun to build a large center near Trenton, and the Atlanta, Georgia, community has bought land for the building to be constructed near the Georgia Institute of Technology. These facilities usually consist of a mosque, or a place for communal prayer, and whatever offices, classrooms and meeting halls are needed to carry on a wide range of cultural and educational activities.

2. Since 1963, Muslim students from overseas studying in North American colleges and universities have been organized into The Muslim Students' Association of the United States and Canada, which has its central office in Plainfield, Indiana. Far from being simply a social grouping to make student years in America easier and more pleasant, the MSA is an active political force. It has espoused the cause of Islamic resurgence and shows considerably more interest in world politics and in issues of social justice than do most of the more settled immigrant communities. But it is quite different to work for Islamic revival in the United States and Canada, where Muslims are a tiny minority of the population and where secularism holds sway, than it is to make such efforts in the Muslim majority countries from which many of these students come. The MSA, with its hundred or more chapters on campuses across the land, its active programs of publishing and teaching, its periodic conferences and its political activism, is in the forefront of the Muslim effort to express Islam faithfully within North American culture.

3. An important Muslim group in America was called until recently the American Muslim Mission. This movement was

born in the 1920s as a protest by American blacks against white supremacy. The religion of Islam was taken as the ideological framework for resistance to white racism. At the beginning little of Islam except its name, the Nation of Islam, was adopted by the movement. Outsiders called its members "Black Muslims," a name that is still used, but which the community disavows. In the 1970s, a change in leadership brought about a gradual revision of emphasis and orientation. The new direction of the movement is reflected in the names it has adopted in recent years. When it ceased to use "Nation of Islam," the group for some time called itself the American Bilalian Community (referring to Bilal, the first black adherent to Islam at the time of the Prophet). Then it changed its name to the World Community of Islam in the West and later to the American Muslim Mission. Now, most groups in this movement prefer simply to be known as American Muslims.

Over the years the movement has drawn closer to Islam as followed by the majority of its believers in the world. Especially under their present leader, Imam Warith Deen Muhammad, these American Muslims have sought contact with their fellow believers in other countries and have taught their members the

---

An American Muslim

Of the many Americans, especially black Americans, who have become Muslims, the most widely known are those whose fame is based on their skills in a variety of sports. In a recent interview, Muhammad Ali talked about what his religion means to him:

Ali's overriding interest now is correcting what he feels is the public misapprehension of Islam. "The average American only knows about Palestinian guerrillas and all the trouble from Khomeini and Qaddafi and hijackers—but that's not what Islam is about. It's about peace and brotherhood."

He distributes a book called "Prayer and Al-Islam," the American Muslim Mission's explanation of its dogma. Recently revised, it shuns the racial and nationalist antagonisms that typify many of the sects.... In this book ... Imam Warithuddin Muhammad ... "urges his followers to fulfill their obligations as citizens of the United States as a matter of conscience, and to accept the burdens of the nation's defense as any other citizen. . . ." He calls for establishing "direct and genuine inter-faith dialogue between leaders of Al-Islam, Christianity and Judaism...."

"Ali: Still Magic," by Peter Tauber, *The New York Times Magazine,* July 17, 1988, Copyright © 1988, The New York Times Co. Reprinted by permission.

prescriptions of the shari'a. Because almost all of its adherents have come to Islam from American Christian backgrounds, this group stands somewhat apart from the immigrant communities, although communication between the two groupings is growing. From Chicago, the American Muslims publish a widely circulated newspaper, *The Muslim Journal*. Their movement works diligently to alleviate urban social problems, to rehabilitate prisoners and to educate its children. This group maintains more than two hundred *masajid*, or mosques.

Some former members of the Nation of Islam have chosen to develop dissenting organizations, holding, with varied emphases, to teachings of the late Elijah Muhammad, their leader from the 1950s and 1960s. One such community still calls itself the Nation of Islam. Another small indigenous Muslim group follows the teaching of Sheikh Daoud Ahmed Faisal (1892-1980). Known as the Islamic Mission of America, it first appeared in the 1920s, in Brooklyn, New York. At present its members have much in common with other American Muslims.

Several associations draw together various groups of Muslims in North America. In June 1981, the Islamic Society of North America was launched as an umbrella organization, federating such groups as the Muslim Students' Association of the United States and Canada and the Muslim Community Association as well as associations of Muslim social scientists, scientists, engineers and medical professionals. The Muslim World League is an international organization dedicated to strengthening Islam in all countries, especially where Muslims are in the minority. With an office in New York City, its personnel maintain close links with both the immigrant communities and other American Muslims. The League provides literature, financial aid and other services. Among the oldest North American organizations is the Federation of Islamic Associations in the United States and Canada, with offices in Redford Township, Michigan. In the USA, the Council of Masajid (mosques) directs an effort at nationwide coordination of Muslim activities.

The Struggle for Identity amid Pluralism

As loyal citizens who are deeply grateful for the freedom of religion in the U.S. and Canada, many Muslims are also caught in contradictions between some aspects of North American life and the teachings of Islam. So they feel that to maintain a clear religious identity requires vigilance and perseverance at all levels of life. For example, Islam does not view itself as a religion set apart as a separate institution from the rest of society. Instead,

Islam incorporates all society in unitary obedience to God. But Muslims in North America discover that Christian churches do function as separate institutions with distinct religious purposes. As a religious minority, Muslims feel tremendous pressure to evolve such an institutional mentality by changing the role of prayer leader and teacher to correspond to the role of the Christian minister; by acquiring substantial buildings for their activities and starting to depend on these buildings and activities to symbolize their identity; and in general, by narrowing the scope of their religious expression to the times of worship.

In some cases for Muslims the distinction between the all-embracing vision of Islam and the current sacred-secular dichotomy in the United States and Canada is somewhat blurred. On the other hand, many Muslim leaders strive to counter the threat of secular fragmentation in North America by upholding the normative Islamic insight of the integrated life under God. Muslim families face this deep problem of identity in the intimacy of their home. They want to protect their children from current North American standards of personal and social morality that conflict with the shar'ia. They want to encourage marriages within the faith, but when young people marry non-Muslims, they need to know how to guide the couple to spiritual stability.

Islam is not yet fully recognized as a religious minority in North America, although Canada is more advanced in this regard than the USA. Because religious consciousness on this continent is extremely individualistic, most people, if they have noticed Muslims at all, have tended to regard them simply as belonging to the multitude of religious "curiosities" that constitute our highly pluralistic society. Muslims want official recognition of their religious identity by the civil authorities in order to provide for the nurture of Muslims in prison and in the military; to be granted free time at work for prayer and for Islamic holidays; to have their special dietary needs, marriage and burial customs, and economic ideals recognized. In a word, the North American Islamic community is not content with a private existence. It aspires to fulfill the historical role of Islam, that is, to embody the divine guidance as contained in the

---

Recently Muslims brought suit against the New Jersey State Department of Corrections because they claimed that the State had denied them the right to attend services of worship while they were incarcerated. The case went all the way to the U.S. Supreme Court, and the Muslims lost. *RMS*

Qur'an and the sunna (example of the Prophet) in the full range of human activities. Muslims do not all agree about the degree to which Islamic principles should be practiced in North American society. However, most feel that this continent, by virtue of its democratic tradition, provides a particularly hospitable environment for carrying out Islamic ideals. So, North American Muslims ask for full acceptance and understanding from the Christian majority.

Peace

In the Qur'an Islam is called the religion of peace: "O You who believe, enter into total peace" (Sura "The Cow," No. 2, verse 208). The word translated "peace" comes from one of the great and fertile roots of the Islamic vocabulary. All Arabic words are formed from groups of three (sometimes four) consonants. The three sounds that make up a root suggest a range of meaning embracing several related ideas. So the root in question, which is *s-l-m*, refers to peace, security, safety, soundness, wholeness, salvation, certainty, etc. Readers of the Bible will recognize the root *s-l-m* as being related to the Hebrew root, *sh-l-m*, from which the well-known biblical word, *shalom*, is formed. The word translated "peace" in the Qur'anic verse above is *silm*. Another form, even more common, is *salam*. The richness of its root meanings make "peace" in Islam much more than the absence of war: it is a state of well-being involving all of life now and in the hereafter.

God is named in the Qur'an by a variety of attributes, which are used when worshipers make supplication, or when they meditate upon the truth of the divine. The attributes are called God's "Beautiful Names," and one of them is "Peace." "There is no god except God [whose name is]...Peace" (Sura "The Gathering," No. 59, verse 23). The Prophet Muhammad is quoted as saying, "O God, you are peace and peace comes from you!" A verb from the same root means "to save" or "to deliver" from evil or danger. Muslims believe that because peace comes from God it consists of a deliverance from all that would hinder peace. "God saves" and "God gives peace" can be expressed by exactly the same two words.

To emphasize the community feeling in Islam, the same word, "to give peace" carries the meaning "to greet" when it is used with a certain preposition. To greet someone is to wish them peace. The noun "peace" also means "greeting." The etiquette of greeting is a religious duty. The Qur'an commands that greetings of peace should be extended: "When you enter a house greet each other with blessed and kindly salutation from God" (Sura "Light," No. 24, verse 61). The sunna of the Prophet gives examples of how a small number of people should wish peace to a larger group, a young person to an elder, a passer-by to one seated and a rider to one walking. All should be greeted, whether they are acquaintances or not. The "spread" of peace by greeting correctly is a duty for all believers. Whenever Muslims answer the telephone, they say first of all, "Peace be with you!" The blessing of peace is even a part of the ritual prayer, salat. And the Qur'an says that angels will welcome the blessed into Paradise with greetings of peace (Sura "Thunder," No. 13, verses 23, 24).

With regard to peace between nations, Islam holds that true peace can never be achieved until all people become Muslims. As long as any part of the world does not accept the advantages and responsibilities of participation in the umma, the danger of conflict is potentially present. Realistically, though, Muslims recognize that the division between Islamic and non-Islamic peoples is likely to continue for a long time. So the political and legal prescriptions of jurisprudence (fiqh) contain provisions for maintaining treaties and peaceful diplomatic relations with non-Muslim states. On this basis Islamic countries feel free to cooperate in the efforts of the United Nations to promote world peace. Armed conflicts between Muslim countries, such as the protracted Iraq-Iran war of the 1980s, are categorically condemned by Islamic law, even though both sides in the conflict claimed to be acting in defense of Islam.

Obedience to Divine Law

Muslims understand the divine will to be revealed in the form of concrete commandments. Islamic law gives believers precise directions on how to be righteous, pure, humble, just and charitable. No higher activity is possible for human beings, according to the Islamic view, than practical obedience to God's law. The gift of that law to humankind is seen as a grace, an act of mercy springing from divine initiative. So to call Islam an oppressive system of legalism, as some Christians have done, is to miss the whole emphasis of the shari'a, considered the path to fullness of life. Yet the shari'a, with its sources in the Qur'an and the hadith, as inclusive as they are, cannot be expected to

At a mosque in Djenne, Mali, West Africa. Photo by John Isaac, U.N. Photo 154730.

cover every human activity. So Muslims accept two other principles, sometimes called sources, but better understood as *tools*
for applying the details of the principles.

The use of analogy and consensus are the tools by which
Muslims have been able to broaden the application of the shari'a
considerably. The ancient authorities who applied analogy and
sought consensus to solve new problems and situations that
arose in the community wrote many volumes on Islamic law.
These writings have provided the basis for life and worship
during many centuries. At the present, debates are occuring
across the Muslim world over how the fiqh of previous centuries
can be adapted to modern conditions. However, many Muslims
would say that the shari'a, that gift of God to humankind, needs
no adjusting to modern conditions. It is unchangeable, and if it
is not being followed today, that is because it is the world, not
the shari'a, that needs to be changed. From these remarks we
can begin to understand that law and obedience to law are
absolutely primary to Muslim thinking. In fact, as we saw in
Chapter 2, the *practice* of the faith and discussion of that practice
occupy in Islam the central place which in Christianity is given
to theology. Muslims theologize also, but that activity takes a
definite second place to concern for the shari'a and its applications in life.

Mercy

A distinguished Moroccan Muslim scholar traveling in Europe
by train found himself seated beside a young Christian who
engaged him in conversation about religion. The Christian said
to the Muslim, "Christianity is a religion of love. What is
yours?" The scholar replied that while he was not accustomed
to categorizing his religion in such terms, he could call Islam a
religion of benevolence, or of justice, or of peace. And, he could
have added, a religion of mercy. Few words better express better
the spirit and devotion of Muslim peoples. Only the strong can
show mercy: the rich toward the poor, the judge toward the
criminal, the creditor toward the debtor, the calm toward the
agitated, the whole person toward one who is disabled. And,
supremely, God is merciful toward creation. Mercy is a godlike
quality. Muslims are intensely God-conscious, God-centered.
There is no area of life outside divine control and, more often
than not, the influence exerted upon human life by God is that
of mercy.

The Eyes of Faith

Al-Shadhili, the North African mystic (died 1258 A.D.) taught that
there is no need for proofs of God's existence. The existence of
God is, said Al-Shadhili, a basic presupposition. To be human is
to know that God is. He added:

If the world contains things whose existence is so obvious
as to need no proof, how much more should the One who
brought those things into being not need proof for his
existence.

How can we know by intellectual proofs the One by whom
we are able to know at all?

How can we prove by examples or concepts the existence
of the One who was before all examples or concepts?

Are creatures or concepts so clear that they can illumine
God? Do they exist parallel with him?

How can examples reveal God [by proofs], when God is
the One who revealed them [in creation]?

We see God only with the eyes of faith; and thereby we
have no need of proof. (*Translation by RMS*)

Muslims learn about God's mercy in the Qur'an. The most
important Arabic word conveying "mercy" is *rahma*; it occurs
114 times in the Qur'an. Muslims say that God acts in mercy
because He is The Merciful One. The double title for God, "The
Merciful, the Compassionate," occurs as an invocation at the
beginning of every sura except one. God creates in mercy,
according to the Muslim Scripture (Sura "The Criterion," No. 25,
verses 47-49). Creation, a continual process, occurs by God's
pure favor and kindness. Human beings cannot measure up to
those extraordinary qualities. The Qur'an constantly reminds
them how limited they are in comparison to the divine majesty.

[God] created human beings from a drop of sperm, but
those same beings became blatant disputers. Cattle are
for you, to make you warm and to give you other
benefits, such as food. They are beautiful as you drive
them home in the evening and as you take them out
to pasture in the morning. They carry your loads to
lands that you could never reach otherwise, unless with
great difficulty. Truly your Lord is kind and merciful.
...He has created other things of which you know
nothing [and the passage goes on to mention fields,
crops, sun, moon and hills].   (Sura "The Bee," No.
16, verses 3-8)

In general, Muslims prefer not to discuss the nature of God. They address Him by His attributes that are listed in the Qur'an, without trying to speculate on exact explanations of these qualities. In fact, many Muslims consider theological discussion irreverent. However, they allow some commentary about the spiritual experience of the believer. One example is the case of the parallel truths of God's mercy and God's wrath. The Qur'an says, "Your Lord has prescribed for Himself mercy" (Sura "Cattle," No. 6, verse 54). This is taken to mean that God does not hasten to punish sinners, but accepts their repentance and is compassionate even toward those who reject Him. One of the hadith texts quotes the Lord as saying, "My mercy has triumphed over my wrath." A rationalist theologian might say that such language must be purely figurative, because both God's mercy and God's wrath are eternal and unchangeable. It is therefore not logically possible for one to win over the other. Some Muslim theologians have expressed this opinion.

Prayers for Refuge

This kind of prayer emphasizes the believer's need for protection from evils that threaten from within and without, and for the ultimate protection of God's own mercy from God's judgment.

...I take refuge with Thee O God from unprofitable knowledge and from a heart without reverence, and from an ever-demanding self, and from unheard petition. From these four I take refuge with Thee.

I take refuge with Thee from hunger, the worst of bedfellows, and from treachery that ruins friendship, and I take refuge with Thee from the evil suggestions of the breast and from the frustration of affairs and the temptation of the grave....

From a prayerbook ascribed to Muhammad al-Fathi al-Marrakushi.

I take refuge with Thy good pleasure from Thy wrath, and with Thy pardon from Thy punishment, and I take refuge with Thee from Thyself.

O God we take refuge with Thy friendship from Thy aversion, with Thy nearness from Thy distance, and we take refuge with Thee from Thee.

From a prayer ascribed to 'Abd al-qadar al-Jilani; The first part of this prayer is attributed to the the Prophet Muhammad.

Both prayers from *Muslim Devotions.* © Constance E. Padwick 1961, reproduced by permission of SPCK, London.

But many other theologians, speaking out of their religious experience and holding strictly to the Qur'an, say that mercy is the unchangeable, eternal attribute of God, while wrath is a quality that depends on the deeds and attitudes of human beings. The fact that mercy triumphs over wrath is, to them, proof that mercy is the greater quality. Mercy is extended even when people do not deserve it, whereas God's wrath is unleashed only on those who deserve it. Mercy envelops human beings even in the embryonic state, before they have the capacity to perform works of obedience. In contrast, people never encounter divine wrath unless they commit blameworthy deeds.

Another hadith text written in the form of a prayer expresses the profound relationship between wrath and mercy: "I take refuge from yourself [O God,] in yourself." This means that, while conscious of its guilt for having committed sins incurring divine wrath, the soul nevertheless trusts in the mercy that is found in the same divine source from which issues righteous anger. The soul's hope is in the mercy that triumphs over wrath.

Mercy is all-encompassing: "Our Lord, you include all things in your mercy and your knowledge" (Sura "The Believer," No. 40, verse 7). At the same time, a special promise of mercy covers those who do good deeds of faith: "I ordain mercy for those who follow me, who give zakat, who believe in our revelations, and who follow the messenger" (Sura "The Heights," No. 7, verse 156). Muslims see no contradiction between divine mercy that is all-encompassing and that which is restricted to believers, since the latter is a special gift to those who are praiseworthy because of their deeds. They are the ones for whom divine mercy is a living hope: "Truly, those who believed, who emigrated and who struggled in the path of God, they are the ones who hope in God's mercy. God is the Forgiving One, the Merciful One" (Sura "The Cow," No.2, verse 218). The mention of forgiveness in this verse is an indication that mercy is linked with the forgiveness of sins in Islam: "O my servants, you who have lived dissipated lives to your own hurt, do not despair of divine mercy. God forgives all sins" (Sura "The Troops," No. 39, verse 53).

Conversely, unbelief, or lack of faith, is in itself a measure of judgment, because it deprives a person of hope in divine mercy: "Those who disbelieve in the revelations of God, and in the meeting with Him, they are the ones who despair of my mercy" (Sura "The Spider," No. 29, verse 23).

Several other verses from the Qur'an illustrate the central

place of mercy in Islamic thinking: "Mercy is good news from God" (Sura "Repentance," No. 9, verse 21). "Jesus is a sign of divine mercy" (Sura "Mary," No. 19, verse 21). "Muhammad is a mercy for all humanity" (Sura "The Prophets," No. 21, verse 107).

With such overwhelming emphasis upon divine mercy in the world and in the lives of Muslims, it is not surprising that Muslims are inspired to be merciful toward their fellow human beings. "Tell those who believe to be forgiving toward those who have no hope in the day of God" (Sura "Kneeling," No. 45, verse 14). "Be forgiving and patient. Do you not wish that God should forgive you? God is the Forgiving One, the Merciful One" (Sura "Light," No. 24, verse 22). A hadith of the Prophet says, "Whoever is not merciful will not receive mercy. Be merciful toward the people of this world, and the One who is in heaven will be merciful to you." One of the great spiritual teachers of Islam exhorted his readers to have mercy on those who are sinful, seeking to turn them to God by exhortation and gentle counsel. And with regard to the needy, the believers, full of mercy, will do their best to supply their needs. If they cannot do so themselves, they will remember the needy in prayer and by sympathy with their unfortunate lot will try to share in their suffering and deprivation.

The word *rahma* (mercy) and its derivatives are used constantly in the everyday speech of Muslims, especially of those who speak Arabic. A more extended version of the greeting of peace, already cited, is: "May peace be with you and the mercy of God." One of many expressions meaning "Thank you" is "May God be merciful to your parents." After the mention of a deceased person, it is said, "May God have mercy upon him (or her)." A deceased person may also be referred to by the phrase, "The object of divine mercy." Both names for God, The Merciful and The Compassionate, derive from the same root as *rahma*. And one of the honorific names given to the city of Medina in Arabia is "The object of divine mercy."

Having described in this and previous chapters something of the coherent structure of the way of Islam, we turn in the next chapter to questions of comparison between the faiths of Muslims and Christians.

5

When Christians and Muslims Meet

*A*lthough the purpose of this book is to present the fundamentals of Islam as a way of life, it is also concerned with relationships, specifically with relationships between Muslims and Christians. I wrote in Chapter 1 that "it is important to learn about Islam in order to be faithful Christian witnesses in the encounter between the church and Muslim peoples." All human interactions are potentially important and enriching in themselves; they can help us to learn about other people, to eliminate misunderstanding, to cooperate to make life more humane. But for Christians all goals are summed up, validated and integrated in the great purpose of rendering a true witness to God as revealed in Jesus Christ. I think it has become clear in the preceding chapters that Muslims affirm a similarly all-encompassing purpose for their lives.

As another step toward making present Christian-Muslim relationships clearer and easier, it will help to examine some of the features of Muslim-Christian encounters in the past. Our efforts to promote such relationships represent the continuation of thirteen centuries of experience. Much can be learned from the remote and the more recent past of Muslim-Christian interactions.

Contest for World Power

Through the centuries the encounter of Islam and Christianity has been indelibly marked by struggles to gain and maintain world power—militarily, politically and economically. After the death of Muhammad in 632 A.D., a mighty push of violent expansionism began as the Arab armies marched against a good part of the known world of that time. Soldiers and statesmen were inspired by the political unity in Arabia newly achieved through Islam. Led by several military geniuses, they were attracted by the prospect of rich booty in the areas outside their barren homeland. Their immediate adversaries, the Byzantines and the Persians (see page 23), still possessed potentially powerful forces, but many years of fighting among themselves had depleted their strength. The Byzantines faced other enemies in the Balkans to the north, and their vassal states surrounding Arabia were restive. Syria, Egypt, Mesopotamia, Transcaucasia,* Persia and Khurasan all fell into Muslim hands well before the end of the seventh century. Early in the eighth century, all of North Africa and a large part of Spain came under the control of Muslim armies. In central Asia, Afghanistan and Transoxania† were conquered and Muslim forces began to penetrate India.

Some of these military conquests were accomplished fairly quickly, but a rapid recital of Islam's victories omits decades of struggle to achieve political and economic supremacy in the conquered lands. The Muslim expansion during the century and a half after the death of the Prophet was one of the more amazing achievements in what we call the medieval period of history.

As the Islamic armies pushed north and west out of Arabia, they won control over many centers of the most highly advanced civilizations of the day, which were Christian in religion. Farther east, in Persia and elsewhere, the populations were not predominantly Christian. For all Islam's resoundingly successful advances to the north and west, important areas of Christendom remained unsubdued: the north of Spain, France, England, the rest of northern Europe and especially the Byzantine stronghold of Constantinople. Consequently, all through the centuries of Muslim supremacy, constant pressure was exerted on the Empire by these unconquered, and incidentally, Christian, centers of power. The Muslim and Christian powers struggled to gain and to control the Mediterranean Sea lanes and the islands of Corsica, Sardinia and Sicily.

Beginning in the eleventh century, the wars of the Crusades continued for nearly two centuries. Through these military expeditions, Christian Europe sought to win the Holy Land back from the Muslims. The Crusades were not directed primarily against Islam as a religion, since its beliefs and practices were

---

* Transcaucasia is an area east of the Black Sea and south of the Caucasus Mountains, now in the USSR. Khurasan is an area now in northeast Iran.

† Transoxania is a crescent-shaped area stretching south and east of the Aral sea. It includes the city of Samarkand and is now within the Kazakh SSR in the Soviet Union.

Muslims and Christians in the World (Estimated, 1985)

REGION	POPULATION	MUSLIMS			CHRISTIANS		
		Number	% of population	% of all Muslims	Number	% of population	% of all Christians
The Middle East	151,490,000	143,468,000	94.70	16.04	3,991,000	2.63	0.30
North Africa	103,900,000	97,085,000	93.44	10.35	5,175,000	5.00	0.35
South Asia	1,003,800,000	284,492,000	28.34	31.80	33,460,000	3.40	2.24
East & Central Asia & U.S.S.R	1,522,579,000	63,644,000	4.28	7.11	122,278,000	8.00	8.17
Mainland South-east Asia	158,585,000	3,840,000	2.42	0.43	7,090,000	4.50	0.47
Insular South-east Asia & Oceania	262,896,000	158,496,000	60.29	17.71	87,010,000	33.10	5.81
Sahelian Tier of African Countries	91,650,000	56,222,000	61.30	6.22	24,200,000	26.60	1.62
Southern Africa	345,257,000	71,576,000	20.73	8.00	187,509,000	54.31	12.53
Eastern Europe	162,912,000	7,739,000	4.75	0.87	127,771,000	78.43	7.86
Western Europe	326,097,000	5,348,000	1.64	0.60	286,622,000	87.89	19.79
North America	265,066,000	3,157,000	1.19	0.26	234,043,000	88.30	15.63
Caribbean & Central America	136,374,000	200,000	.15	0.02	126,777,000	93.00	8.47
South America	265,309,000	811,000	.30	0.09	251,091,000	94.60	16.77
Totals	4,795,915,000	896,078,000	18.68	100.0	1,497,017,000	31.21	100.0

Table I. "Muslims and Christians in the World," reprinted from *Christians and Muslims Together: An Exploration by Presbyterians*, edited by Byron L. Haines and Frank L. Cooley. © The Geneva Press, 1987. Used by permission.

largely unknown to Europeans. Their objective was to oppose an alien power, vaguely called "heathen," because it held a land supremely significant to Christians. After the Crusades, fifteenth-century Spanish and Portuguese Christians instigated military incursions of more limited scope against western strongholds of Islam in what are now Morocco, Algeria and Tunisia. Constantinople was eventually overcome by the Turkish Muslims in 1453, and the military and political strength of the Turkish Ottoman Empire was sufficient to maintain an uneasy balance of power with Europe for several centuries.

Then, when Christendom, as embodied by the countries of Europe, awakened to a period of scientific discovery and colonial empire building in the seventeenth, eighteenth and nineteenth centuries, Muslim populations had a turn at resisting intruders. Again, the fact that the conquered peoples belonged to the Islamic religion was of little importance to European colonizers. They were simply seeking to build empires.

In summary, when Muslim peoples and Christian peoples found themselves in conflict through the ages, their antagonism was not based primarily on differences of religion, even though they often perceived and designated their conflicts as "religious" wars. In fact, each side saw the other simply as an obstacle to the free exercise of political and economic power. (The new and often alarming turn that the contest for world power has taken in the last half of the twentieth century will receive special attention in Chapter 6.)

Cultural Isolation

Because Christians and Muslims have so often set themselves as adversaries through the centuries, the people on each side have for the most part lived in isolation from those on the other. In areas like Damascus and Jerusalem, where Muslims ruled and Christians lived as a minority, much cooperation existed between the two groups in business, government and professional life. But because of the status of protected citizen (dhimmi, described in Chapter 3), the minority became socially isolated. At the international level Muslims and Christians seldom met. Soldiers, sailors and traders were most consistently in touch with each others' societies. In view of their long isolation from personal encounters, it is not surprising that both Muslim and Christian communities nourished negative attitudes toward those they considered as threatening enemies.

Religious Controversy

In view of the power struggle involving armies and rulers, the two religions inevitably became involved in conflicts of belief and practice. Religious conflict was in turn used as an ideological weapon to insure a decisive stand against the enemy. If the ruling powers of one side could convince its people that the others were heretics or heathen, the fervor of military or political opposition could be heightened.

The Muslim View of Christian Beliefs

From the beginning Muslims had a well-defined idea of Christianity. Some understanding of Christian faith was indispensable to Muslims' affirmation of their own religious identity. In the first place, Islam developed several centuries later than Christianity, and it appeared in an area of the world already influenced by Christians. From the outset it could not ignore the church. In the second place, the Christians of Arabia refused to accept the Prophet Muhammad in spite of the fact that Muhammad proclaimed the prophethood of Jesus. So as Islam developed it faced the task of explaining to itself why Christians did not accept the prophethood of Muhammad.

The Muslim view of Christianity includes much that is positive. Jesus is believed to be the divinely sent, virgin-born, sinless, miracle-working Prophet to his people, the one to whom God revealed the Gospel *(Injil)*. Of Mary the mother of Jesus, the Qur'an says, "Into the chaste one [Mary] we breathed of our spirit and we made her and her son a sign for all creatures" (Sura "The Prophets," No. 21, verse 91). Jesus is called in the Qur'an "a word from God," "Messiah," a "messenger to the Children of Israel," and "a spirit from God." None of these statements contradicts Christian teachings. Although Christians may not commonly think of Jesus in terms of prophethood, he referred to himself as a prophet in sayings like that of Matthew 13:57: "A prophet is not without honor except in his own country and in his own house." According to the Muslim view, Jesus' life and teachings were so pure and so impressive that he aroused the opposition of wicked men who sought to destroy him. As they were carrying out their intent to crucify him, God intervened in a mighty act of deliverance, taking the Prophet Jesus to paradise. The Qur'an puts it this way: "They did not kill him, nor did they crucify him, but it only seemed so to them. . . . God exalted him unto Himself" (Sura "The Women,"

Empires: Powers and Arts

Six blue and white wall tiles from fifteenth-century Turkey or Syria. Depending on location, this artistry would have developed in the powerful empire of the Mamluks, who ruled Syria and Egypt in the thirteenth and fourteenth centuries or the even more powerful empire of the Ottoman (Turkish) rulers, who conquered the Mamluks in the early fifteenth century in the course of the expansion of their empire outward in all directions from Turkey and the Grecian peninsula.

The classic Islamic style of ornamentation called the *arabesque* developed from such patterns of intertwining leaves and branches, arranged to form endless geometric variations that filled entire surfaces with pattern. Photo: all rights reserved, The Metropolitan Museum of Art, Rogers Fund, 1967. (67.69.1-6)

No. 4, verses 157, 158). The Muslim Christ is alive, and according to a tradition of the faith he will return to earth at the end of the age to be the instrument of God's judgment and to establish the universal sway of Islam.

In addition to setting aside the historical reality of the crucifixion, the Qur'an denies two of Christianity's faith claims. It rejects the divine Sonship of Jesus: "The Christians say that the Messiah is the Son of God. . . . How they have perverted the truth!" (Sura "Repentance," No. 9, verse 30). It also rejects the doctrine of the Trinity: "Those who say that God is the third of three have surely disbelieved" (Sura "The Table," No. 5, verse 73).

Although it specifically disclaims these central Christian doctrines, the Qur'an contains a warm appreciation of Christian people: "The people who are nearest in friendship to the believers are those who say, 'We are Christians,' because among them are priests and monks, and they are not proud" (Sura "The Table," No. 5, verse 82). Also, the Scriptures given to Moses and to Jesus are held up as divinely inspired: "[God] sent down to you [Muhammad] the Scripture in truth, confirming that which came before it, and He revealed the Torah and the Gospel" (Sura "The Family of 'Imran," No. 3, verse 3).

Muslims believe that Christians early fell into error because they were not faithful to the original revelation of the Gospel through the Prophet Jesus. It is said that the early Christians quarreled among themselves over the proper interpretation of the Gospel, and that they made Jesus into a divine figure. They also tampered with the original Scriptures so that the Bible which Christians read today is not the same as the Scriptures that were first revealed. In summary, we can say that the Qur'an is not entirely anti-Christian in tone, even though it contains strong reproaches addressed to Christians and some clear rejections of Christian doctrine. This acceptance and respect, tempered with disapproval, has marked the Muslim attitude toward Christians down to the present.

The Christian View of Islamic Beliefs

Christians, receivers of the earlier revelation, had no place for Islam in their system. When the Muslim armies began to take control of Christian populations, Christians were completely ignorant of what the new conquerors' religion represented. In places like Egypt, Palestine and Syria, the Muslims were often welcomed as deliverers from the military and religious yoke of the ruling Greeks from Byzantium.

When some information began to be gained about Muslims' beliefs, many Christians, especially scholars, regarded Islam with disdain. The warriors from the desert were unlettered, and their religion was not to be taken seriously. Other Christians judged Muslims to be heretics who would finally be brought to the way of orthodox Christianity. Not many years passed, though, before the conquered Christian populations became aware of at least the main points of Muslim opposition to the beliefs and practices of the church.

The Era of Polemics

The lack of source material makes it difficult to retrace the exchanges between Christians and Muslims in the early years of their meeting. One of the earliest records of Christian reaction to Muslim accusations of false doctrine is in the polemical writings by John of Damascus, a learned theologian who died about 755. Accustomed to religious controversy, Christians had perfected the use of philosophical arguments to refute the Jews and pagans who opposed Christianity. John of Damascus tried to prove the deity of Christ and to answer the accusations of the Muslims. He also launched an attack against them and their beliefs, thus inaugurating a process of attack and counterattack that has characterized the encounter between Christians and Muslims with regularity through the centuries. John considered Muhammad to have been a heretic, and he cast aspersions upon the morality of the Muslim way. The fact that this polemicist could write in such a way while being subject, with his people, to the dhimmi status in Islam is evidence of the freedom of discussion permitted by the Muslim rulers. Yet such theological writings were probably not widely read, so they did not have repercussions among the masses.

It is said that Emperor Leo III of Byzantium entered the theological controversy in the early eighth century by replying to a letter written to him by Caliph 'Umar II, attacking Christianity. From the reply attributed to Leo III we learn that Muslims also accused Christians of ignoring prophecies about the coming of Muhammad that they considered to be contained in the Bible and of abandoning features of the divine law contained in the Bible, such as circumcision and the observance of the Sabbath.

The Vocabulary of Religious Argument

Polemic derives from *polemos*, the Greek word for "war." A polemic is an aggressive attack on or refutation of another's principles or opinions. Polemics is the art or practice of this aggressive style of argument, especially as a method of conducting theological controversy. (The opposite practice, of peacefully persuasive discussion, is called "irenics.")

Apologetics derives from *logos*, Greek for "word, thought, reason," and means the method of making a formal "apology" in its older sense of "defense" of a person, doctrine or course of action. It applies especially to an argumentative defense of one's faith.

Muslims pointed out that Jesus did not come to destroy the law, but to fulfill it.

When the center of Muslim culture moved from Damascus to Baghdad in the mid-eighth century, exchanges of polemical attacks continued. Christian philosophers, scientists and churchmen were active in the intellectual life of the Empire (see map, page 23). Several writings from Christian apologists of the late eighth and ninth centuries have been preserved, including those of Timothy, Patriarch of the Nestorian Church; Abu Qurra, a bishop of the Melkite Church; and an almost unknown Nestorian scholar named 'Ammar al-Basri. These writings, all in direct response to Muslim arguments, reflect a high level of reasoning, philosophical and biblical. They do not make exaggerated attacks against the Muslims, but strongly defend those points of doctrine under attack. It would have been well if other apologists had imitated them, but the further removed apologists were from the scene of actual daily encounter between Muslims and Christians, the more they tended to distort the position of their adversaries. In the ninth century, for example, Nicetas of Byzantium, writing from the shelter of his Greek environment, made vituperative attacks against the Qur'an, Muhammad and Muslim doctrine. He was one of the first to deny that Muslims worship the true God.

In subsequent centuries other debates emerged, all having to do with purported weaknesses and errors in the other side's position. Following the example of Christians, Muslims wrote more detailed polemical works. They claimed that the Christian ethic was impractical and too demanding, insisting that Islam's law aims at moderation and that its ethic is attainable by ordinary human beings.

The Crusades increased the willingness of both sides to see weakness and error in the other. In the years following those Christian holy wars to recover the land where Jesus lived, fanciful ideas about Muhammad and the Muslims became current in Europe. Some Christians said that Muhammad was a renegade from the Christian church, that he was an epileptic, that he advocated sexual license in order to destroy the Christian world. Fired by such inflammatory lies, polemicists in the West worked to destroy Islam, either by the power of convincing argument or by the force of arms. Scholars like the twelfth-century Peter the Venerable, who translated the Qur'an into Latin, did not become caught up in the rhetoric of holy war, but nonetheless sought vigorously to discredit both the person of

Muhammad and the law of Islam. This aggressively negative attitude was to dominate Western thought until modern times. Traces of it were still found in the early twentieth century when some statesmen and church leaders predicted the early demise of Islam, presumably as the result of the influence of Western ways of thinking.

From the Muslim side, the critique of Christianity was elaborated through the centuries in reaction to deepening animosity on both sides. For example, one of the most learned as well as most acerbic Muslim critics was the Spaniard, Ibn Hazm (d. 1064). His arguments against Christianity included these points:

> • In view of the multitude of Christian sects with their differing views of the Trinity, it is impossible to take that doctrine seriously.
> • The incarnation of Christ is impossible, because it would introduce innovation in the nature of God.
> • From the New Testament, Jesus is proven to be only a prophet.
> • The crucifixion is under the condemnation of Deuteronomy 21:22-23.
> • There are many divergences between the Septuagint and the Hebrew Old Testament, so these documents, as they exist, are not trustworthy.

Types of Mission

While both Islam and Christianity are missionary religions, the ways in which they have expressed their missionary concern have varied widely from age to age. Reduced to dhimmi status in the East, Christians were not permitted to seek the conversion of their Muslim overlords. Elsewhere, as we have seen, the prevailing Christian sentiment held that Islam was a dangerous force and should be destroyed. Muslims did not, as a rule, seek the conversion of Christians, although they welcomed into Islam any who wanted to change their religion.

A few exceptions stand out to Christians' early general attitude of indifference toward missionary work among the Muslims. In ninth-century Spain, then a part of the Islamic empire, there arose a movement headed by Eulogius, Bishop of Toledo. Its aims conformed to the growing Western Christian idea that Islam must be destroyed. But instead of seeking to put Islam down by force, this movement endeavored quietly to receive Muslim converts into the church. Muslim authorities stopped this movement by executing several of its leaders. Muslims have

History's Long Shadows

In some locations where Muslim and Christian groups clashed centuries ago, bitter memories have never entirely faded. There are places in the Middle East where the medieval European crusaders are still remembered as cruel invaders. In Spain, on the walls of Toledo's church of St. John, above, chains of Christians once imprisoned by the Moors hang as memorials to hostility. This ancient city could provide either roots for resentment or models for toleration. For centuries Toledo was a multicultural center for Christians, Muslims and Jews, first under Muslim (Moorish) rule from 712 to 1085 and then under Christian rule from 1085 to 1492. At that time, Muslims and Jews who refused to convert to Christianity were forced to leave Spain. Photo by *CMA*

usually reacted with vehemence to attempts by Christians to make converts of the people of Islam.

In thirteenth-century Morocco, a group of Franciscan missionaries found the martyrdom they were seeking when they openly invited Muslims to forsake the Prophet Muhammad and come into the church.

The modern missionary movement has had its share of martyrs as well. Usually these deaths have resulted when

Christian missionaries offered extraordinary provocations to Muslim sensibility, such as attacking the character of the Prophet Muhammad.

At various times, some sectors of the church have wished to approach Muslims peaceably for the sake of leading them to become Christians. For example, Pope Gregory IX (1227-1241), wrote to the Almohad king of Morocco:

> *We desire ardently that you acquire, with a pious heart and a humble spirit, grace for this present life and glory for the life to come. . . . We pray that . . . He [God] will show you, who walk in darkness, his only Son, the true light, and I invite you . . . to accept this same Son, the Lord Jesus Christ, so that purified by the waters of baptism you might please the Lord as his adopted son in a new life. . . .*

This statement seems remarkable when we consider that it was issued toward the close of the Crusades, which were motivated by quite a different spirit.

Christians' zeal to make converts was mixed with the desire to discredit Muslim doctrine by rational argument. This mixture of motives, which may seem contradictory to us, governed nineteenth- and twentieth-century missionary work. For example, *The Balance of Truth*, by a German missionary to India and Persia, Karl Pfander, published in 1835, represents this tendency, as do other works of Christian apologetics written to convince Muslims of both the error of Islam and the truth of Christianity.

The colonizing thrust of western Europe in the eighteenth and nineteenth centuries was accompanied by intensive Christian missionary work in several Muslim lands. Such efforts, which extended into the twentieth century and continue among some Christians even now, have been resented by Muslims. They feel that missionaries took advantage of their nations' military forces and economic strengths in order to impose themselves and their religious institutions upon the Muslim world.

A Spirit of Conciliation

The history of Christian-Muslim relations exhibits almost unrelieved conflict—military, political, economic and religious. The Christian world has seemed incapable of promoting and maintaining amicable relations with the Muslim world, most probably because Christians have not found a place for Islam in *their* view of the universe. Christianity is exclusive in teaching that it is the only way of salvation, and up to now the task of being

---

Forerunners for Friendship

As precursors of those who seek Christian-Muslim friendship, the following names come to mind:

Peter the Venerable of twelfth-century Europe, who, in spite of his lack of insight into Muslim beliefs, studied the Qur'an and opposed holy war against Islam.

Al-Ghazali (died 1111), a towering figure of Muslim theology and spirituality, who showed extraordinary tolerance and understanding toward Christians.

Barhebraeus (died 1286), a Syrian bishop of the Jacobite Church, who by his writings and example showed that it was possible to live in positive and fruitful relationships with Muslims.

Roger Bacon (died 1294), a British Franciscan philosopher, who expressed in his writings a positive appreciation of Islam.

Guillaume Postel, a sixteenth-century French churchman with a vision of Christian-Muslim reconciliation.

Adrian Relandus, a Dutch orientalist of the eighteenth century, who was unusually fair in his writing about Islam. *RMS*

---

reconciled with another exclusive system, Islam, has proven too taxing for Christendom.

Nor, from their side, have Muslims been able to overcome their doctrinal and moral objections to Christianity. In spite of the very positive place that Christianity occupies in the Islamic view of the universe, Muslims have stressed their anti-trinitarian feelings so far as to accuse Christians of being polytheists. Of course, neither Christians nor Muslims have been helped to achieve mutual respect by the course of world politics or by the rapacious actions and tendencies of some individuals and groups of people.

In spite of the somber history of Muslim-Christian interaction, a new spirit of conciliation is evident among some Christians and Muslims in the world today. It does not yet govern all or even most encounters between the religions, but it is growing. Neither is this spirit altogether unprecedented (see box on this page).

Perhaps the most important precursors of this new movement were the thousands of ordinary believers in Islam and in Christianity who for centuries lived together as neighbors in several countries, proving by their example that religion does not have to be a factor for animosity between peoples.

Since the Second World War a number of Christians and
Muslims have been working for a spirit of understanding and
reconciliation between members of the two religious communities. This movement is the most recent development in Christian-Muslim relations. On the Christian side, it results in part
from the intensive theological research of the last hundred years,
particularly in Europe. Modern Christian theology has developed in societies that have come to value pluralism of peoples,
opinions and religions, so that a new approach to Islam is able
to thrive. So far, not many Christians have realized the implications of this theological climate for the encounter with Islam,
because Christian-Muslim relations remains an issue of low priority in the Christian churches.

Modern pioneers in Christian-Muslim relations are few; most
of them developed their interest through direct relationships.
Three such persons immediately come to mind. Only one of
them can be called a theoretician of Christian-Muslim relations,
and it was his acquaintance with Muslims that led him to
develop his ideas. Wilfred Cantwell Smith of the United Church
of Canada has through his writings done much to break down
the barriers between persons of faith. His relationships with
Muslims have been his basis for interpreting humankind's religious experience. One of his most compelling theses is that the
modern world, with its intermingling of cultures, affords an
unprecedented opportunity for Christians, in faithfulness to their
missionary motivation, to participate with Muslims as well as
with believers from other religions in the ongoing multiform
religious evolution of humankind.

Louis Massignon (d. 1962) was a French diplomat and scholar
whose life was transformed by his contact with the world of
Islam. His consecration to God as revealed in Christ, within the
Roman Catholic tradition, grew very much in terms of the
Islamic understanding of godliness. In his thought and writings,
Massignon moved constantly back and forth in the most natural
way between Christianity and Islam, yet without ever failing to
appreciate the particularity of each religion. No one has shown
better than he how far a Christian can go in sensitive, self-
sacrificial friendship with Muslims. Only recently have Massignon's writings begun to be translated into English, but French-
speaking Christians in touch with Islam, and a number Muslims
as well, consider Massignon to be a key figure in their spiritual
formation.

From the Anglican branch of Christendom comes the poet-bishop and searcher of the Qur'an, Kenneth Cragg. His brilliant writings have opened new perspectives to a whole generation of Christians. Cragg, a sober philosopher, theologian, and skilled Arabist, is devoted to the church. His life among Muslims in the Middle East as well as his research have led him to feel with exquisite sensibility the theological gulf that separates the two religions. Yet he also has found untold riches of common themes in the Qur'an and in the Bible, in Muslim and Christian theology, in the two contrasting paths of spirituality and in the two separate patterns of worship.

These exceptional individuals and a few others have been pioneers in the movement for a new era in Christian-Muslim relations. Along with them are a number of missionaries and other Christians who have gone far in breaking down barriers of misunderstanding and prejudice by offering themselves in transparent vulnerability as friends to Muslims. Many Muslims have responded in like manner, and a fresh dynamic of relationships is at work today. The movement is not large in scope, and one cannot even say that from the Muslim side any real movement is taking shape. But the promise exists. The future is opening, as barriers fall between believers.

Christian and Muslim Initiatives

A declaration made by the Vatican Council in 1964 marked a turning point in the official Roman Catholic attitude toward Islam:

> *Upon the Muslims, too, the Church looks with esteem. They adore one God, living and enduring, merciful and powerful, creator of the heavens and the earth and speaker to men. They strive to submit wholeheartedly even to his inscrutable decrees, just as did Abraham, with whom the Islamic faith is pleased to associate itself. Though they do not acknowledge Jesus as God, they revere him as prophet. They also honor Mary, his virgin mother; at times they call on her, too, with devotion. In addition, they await the day of judgment when God will give each man his due, after raising him up. Consequently, they prize the moral life and give worship to God especially through prayer, almsgiving and fasting.*
>
> *Although in the course of the centuries many quarrels and hostilities have arisen between Christians and Muslims, this Council urges all to forget the past*

*and to strive sincerely for mutual understanding. On
behalf of all mankind, let them make common cause of
safeguarding and fostering social justice, moral values,
peace and freedom.*

As a result of the official publication of this text and of the
Roman Catholic Church's expressions of interest in other religions, a Secretariat was established at the Vatican to promote
good relationships between Catholics and members of non-
Christian religions. The Secretariat section on Islam has been
very active, publishing a number of materials and organizing
meetings between Christians and Muslims. Personnel competent
to work among the peoples of Islam are trained at several
specialized centers, such as the Pontifical Institute for Arabic and
Islamic Studies in Rome and a few research centers in Muslim
capitals.

Protestants have no similar central body that speaks for their
many churches. The World Council of Churches, a forum for
many Protestant and Orthodox bodies and a means for coopera-
tive effort, has established a division for dialogue with people
of living faiths. This office has organized a variety of gatherings
in Europe, Asia and Africa to encourage exchanges between
Christians and Muslims on many topics. Protestant church
workers who are sent to live among Muslims can receive
appropriate training at the Selly Oak Colleges in Birmingham,
England, and at several institutes in other countries.

In the United States only one center has as its primary aim
the cultivation of constructive, friendly relations between Chris-
tians and Muslims, based on the primacy of faith in God: the
Duncan Black Macdonald Center for the Study of Islam and
Christian-Muslim Relations at Hartford Seminary in Hartford,
Connecticut. *The Muslim World*, a quarterly journal devoted to
Christian-Muslim understanding, is published there. In addition
to the teaching and research staff of the Macdonald Center,
Hartford Seminary offers office space to the Office on Christian-
Muslim Relations sponsored by the National Council of the
Churches of Christ in the USA, with a full-time staff member.
The goal of the office is to help Muslims and Christians in the
United States to enter into mutually beneficial relationships.

Muslims have responded in various ways to Christian initiatives of friendship that are based on mutual respect. In many
cases they have shown joy and relief when they realize that their
Christian acquaintances have abandoned traditionally aggressive
and condescending approaches to them. When they find that

RESOLUTION ON ANTI-ISLAM, ANTI-MUSLIM AND ANTI-ARAB PREJUDICE IN THE UNITED STATES OF AMERICA

The Governing Board of the National Council of the Churches of Christ in the U.S.A., recognizing that the prevalence of stereotyping and prejudice against Islam, Muslims and Arabs and the violence associated with this bigotry should be a matter of great concern to Christians; and in order to help Christians free themselves and their institutions from this racism and ethnic and religious bigotry: calls upon Christians, the churches, and church-related agencies to undertake the following:

(1) To pursue a better understanding of Islam, Muslims, and Arab Christians by including in the churches' educational programs a study of Islam, of the Muslim world and the Christian minorities within that world, and of the issues that have united and divided us by inviting Muslims and Arabs to be a part of the leadership and fellowship of such programs.

(2) To encourage local and regional ecumenical and interfaith agencies to seek conversation and cooperation with Muslim religious organizations.

(3) To advocate and defend the civil rights of Arabs and Muslims living in the U.S. by such means as monitoring organizations and agencies which exercise responsibility for the peace, welfare and security of the community.

(4) To reject the religious and political demogoguery and manipulation manifest in the reporting of events related to the Middle East, to seek an understanding of the underlying causes of the events labeled as "terrorist," and to condemn violence as a means of enforcing national will or achieving peace.

(5) To challenge and rebut statements made about Islam, Muslims, and Arabs that embody religious stereotyping, prejudice and bigotry.

November 6, 1986

they no longer have to defend themselves against the Christians, they are able to express freely the kinship that they feel with them and to explore frankly the differences that exist between the two religions. In several parts of the world, Muslims have taken the initiative to organize interfaith gatherings. At the same time, the pattern of Christian political and economic domination of the recent past is too fresh in the minds of many Muslims for them to welcome easily new overtures from their former adversaries. Sometimes they are puzzled, distrustful and defensive—and naturally so.

Steps in the New Approach to Relationships

The religious difficulties between Christians and Muslims are of two basic kinds: doctrinal and moral. In the interest of conciliation, a value whose importance is self-evident, these two difficulties should be faced frankly and then set aside for awhile for the sake of starting to talk. First, many doctrinal problems can be discussed rationally as issues of the understanding. If we Christians explain carefully what we believe, then Muslims can understand what we say about our doctrines, even if some beliefs have to do with the divine mystery. In the same way, if we Christians simply listen carefully to Muslims, we can understand what they say about their beliefs. That is the first step in meeting the doctrinal problem frankly.

Although the process sounds simple, this careful listening to one another is precisely what has been missing through the ages. For example, the reason Christians have accused Muslims of being fatalistic and enemies of progress is that Christians have seldom paid attention to the delicate interplay between divine sovereignty and human freedom in Islam. Muslims have similarly accused Christians of believing in a Trinity of three gods because Muslims have not listened to Christians discuss the ways in which they understand the Trinity as a unity.

Very often doctrinal points of contention draw people from the two faiths into animated debate. I have seen American Christians become provoked when they first hear Muslim accusations that the church has ignored supposed biblical prophecies of the coming of Muhammad into the world. The immediate temptation is to launch into a rebuttal of such arguments. Instead, we need to remember that we are not the first Christians to be confronted with these and similar accusations. In fact, some of the best minds in Christendom have made rebuttals against Muslim objections. The only thing that rebuttals or counter-accusations accomplish is to underscore the gap between our two faiths. No one has ever "won" the argument.

If we listen to each other we will take a great step toward reconciliation. But listening is only the first step. The doctrinal difficulties between our two peoples are heightened because we want the others not only to understand us but to believe as we do. So, the Muslim says, for example, "If you understand what we mean by the prophethood of Muhammad, why will you not

One Place of Meeting: The Christian Study Centre in Rawalpindi, Pakistan

The idea of establishing a study centre for Christian-Muslim relations was initially discussed in 1951 by the Committee on Islamic Studies (later the Committee for the Study of Religion and Society) of the West Pakistan Christian Council, now the National Council of Churches in Pakistan. With the encouragement, guidance, and support of various ecumenical organizations and individuals, both inside and outside Pakistan, the Christian Study Centre was founded in 1967 as an autonomous, non-profit organization with the explicit purpose of research on and dialogue between Christianity and Islam. Today the centre enjoys the full support of the three Christian churches officially recognized by the government of Pakistan: the Roman Catholic Church, the Church of Pakistan (Anglican, Lutheran, Scottish Presbyterian, and United Methodist), and the Presbyterian Church.

The Christian Study Centre maintains a very fine research library and study room; publishes literature relevant to its purpose, primarily through its bilingual (Urdu and English) journal, *al Mushir*; arranges lectures, discussions, and courses of study on aspects of Christianity and Islam and the relationship between the two; provides resource personnel for conferences, institutes, or seminars sponsored by Christian or Muslim groups; and welcomes visiting scholars from other countries who wish to examine firsthand the situation in Pakistan and its possibilities for understanding and dialogue.

The staff of the Christian Study Centre are Christian, but significant relationships with Muslim scholars are carefully and thoughtfully maintained. Muslims have occasionally given the monthly lecture offered at the Centre. The degree to which Muslim scholars can openly participate is limited by the overall political climate in the country. *KMR*

accept it as true?" And the Christian says to the Muslim, "Your Scriptures say that you should respect and believe in the gospel of Jesus. Why, then, do you not read it?" Therefore, the second step toward meeting doctrinal difficulties frankly is to give up the insistence that the other become like ourselves. To do so does not require abandoning a vital witness to one's faith or the concern that others enter into the joys of salvation. What it does mean is leaving the other person free to be himself or herself.

Once these two steps are taken, the discussion can move to other matters without being blocked by doctrinal differences.

Doctrine is important, but it is not the only question in our relationships. Doctrinal matters should not stand in the way of whatever form or degree of reconciliation is possible.

What about moral issues? It is good to have another religious community to encounter so that our moral choices can be tested by the ethical insights of the other group. We need to be a moral check on each other. An ethical torpor may descend on a people who will not accept criticism from those outside. What is unfortunate about our two religious communities is that we have for many centuries simply hurled accusations of immoral or unethical behavior at each other, each assuming a position of superiority in relation to the other.

Such recrimination offers no lasting benefits. For each moral or ethical defect in one community, a corresponding defect can always be discovered in the other community. As an example, Christians have accused Muslims of unbridled sensuality because they permit polygamy. Muslims, in turn, have pointed out that polygamy as a stable social force is preferable to prostitution and other forms of extramarital sexual involvements that are common in the Christian world. Also, Christians often accuse

---

Talking Together in Milwaukee

In 1980 Lucille Walsh, O.S.F., a professor who teaches courses in Islam and other religions at Cardinal Stritch College in Milwaukee, organized the Islamic-Christian Dialogue of the Diocese of Milwaukee, with the assistance of Dr. Abbas Hamdani, a Muslim university professor. Roman Catholics, Protestants and Muslims (Milwaukee's Muslim community mumbers almost 4,000 persons) have been meeting several times a year in ongoing discussions. Talking together here are Janan (Atta) Waleed Najeed, Sister Lucille Walsh and Trudy Bush. In the boxes on pages 107, 109 and 111 are comments from some participants in the Dialogue.

Photo courtesy of Lucille Walsh, and statements from her article, "The Genesis of an Islamic-Christian Dialogue," *New Catholic World*, Nov.-Dec. 1988. Used by permission.

Muslim nations of being turbulent and warlike, unable to settle their differences among themselves. Muslims point out that it is Christian countries that have fought two world wars in half a century. To make invidious comparisons of our two religious systems in order to prove the moral superiority of one over the other is an exercise in vanity. Therefore, we can safely set aside the moral problem insofar as it consists of picking out the flaws in the other group. The right kind of mutual moral critique will come as a result of meeting together on a deeper level.

Having dealt with the two principal difficulties in the way of our relationships, we are free to concentrate upon the things that draw us together. These elements of common ground will be the subject of Chapter 6.

To close this chapter, here are some questions that Christians often ask about Muslims and Islam. The answers furnished here are an example of what is meant by listening to others, a new approach to interfaith relations.

Questions People Ask About Islam

Question: Is it appropriate to use the words "Mohammedan" and "Mohammedanism"?

Answer: No, because these are not words that Muslims use to describe themselves. Europeans began to call Muslims Mohammedans and the religion, Mohammedanism, by making a

---

From L. Humphrey Walz, Janesville, Wisconsin

The Islamic-Christian Dialogue has heightened my awareness of the kinship of Judaism, Christianity and Islam as *ethical monotheism* distinct from other faiths. It has made me especially aware of the special oneness of Catholicism and Protestantism, when we seek together to live for and under Jesus Christ.

The Muslims, who look on our doctrine of the Incarnation as idolatrous *shirk* and on our doctrine of the trinity as tri-theism, have given us a challenge to think in greater detail—for our own, as well as others' clarification—on the nature of these doctrines.

The fact that the Arabic consonantal cluster SLM, standing for "submission" (to God), through both divine sovereignty and human commitment, occurs in "Islam" (the faith), "Muslim" (the believer) and "Salaam" (the outcome), has led me to fuller appreciation of both the Old Testament (e.g. Isaiah 2:1-4; Micah 4:1-5) and the New Testament (Matthew 5:6-10, etc.) emphases.

L. Humphrey Walz is a Presbyterian minister.

false analogy. They reasoned that since those who worship Christ are called Christians, so those who worship Mohammad are called Mohammedans. Of course, this analogy was wrong on two counts: first, Muslims do not worship Muhammad. And second, outsiders had no right to call Muslims by a name that is not recognized by the people of Islam themselves.

Question: Is the God of Islam the same as the God of Christianity?

Answer: It seems clear that Muslims and Christians worship the same God. Some Christians contest this affirmation, but no Muslims disagree with it. If we do not worship the same God, then we must find another name either for their God or our God. Allah, the word for God in the Qur'an, is the same word that is used by Arab Christians in their religious life. To say that we worship the same God does not mean that we share the same interpretations of the mystery of God's nature. Of course there are enormous differences of understanding.

Question: Can Christians accept Muhammad as a prophet?

Answer: Muslims are sensitive to this question. They say, We Muslims accept Jesus, but you Christians will not accept Muhammad. In answer to the question, Christians generally do not accept Muhammad because they do not know about him. Once they learn the facts of his life and accomplishments, they usually have no difficulty in accepting him as a prophet. He functioned as a prophet. Sympathetic Christian readers of the Qur'an recognize much of its content as corresponding to the truth as they perceive it. Of course, the denials of Christian doctrine in the Qur'an, which were described earlier in this chapter, cannot be accepted by Christians. The most generous explanation that can be given to the rejections of the Trinity and of the cross is that the Qur'anic formulations are directed against false emphases and distorted interpretations of these doctrines rather than against sound Christian beliefs. There is some historical basis for this explanation. Even with such an answer, Christians must confess that the Qur'an does not adequately represent Christianity as they, who believe in it, desire for it to be known. Therefore, they can never accept Muhammad in the same way that Muslims do. If they did, then they would be Muslims, not Christians. In the same way, Muslims, although they are quick to profess belief in Jesus Christ, do not believe in him the way Christians do. If they did, they would be Christians, not Muslims.

Question: Is the paradise of Islam a place of sensual pleasure?

Answer: Yes. Any description of the abode of eternal bliss must be couched in human language. The message of the Qur'an emerged in a dry, hot land, so it is understandable that the place of fullest joy should be described as full of fresh, running water and green grass and trees. Also, paradise in Islam is the place of ultimate and pure enjoyment of all the pleasures of the flesh and spirit that humans know. One of the Christian images of paradise, the Heavenly Jerusalem, is also very sensual: streets of gold, gates of pearl and walls adorned with precious stones (Revelation 21).

Question: Do Muslims believe in sin?

Answer: Yes, but they do not believe in "original sin" as that

---

From Abbas Hamdani, Milwaukee, Wisconsin

In pursuing the goals of our Islamic-Christian Dialogue over these eight years, we informed ourselves by talks and discussions on the history, the doctrines, the society and the concerns of our two religions and religious communities. We met not only intellectually but socially to foster friendship and fellowship and to enjoy each other's holidays and religious occasions.

Our Dialogue has found recognition with and special mention by the Vatican, the World Muslim League, and the World Council of Churches.

Let me cite a verse or our Qur'an about the Christians (V:85):
"And the nearest among them in love
To the Believers (i.e., Muslims) wilt thou
Find those who say,
'We are Christians,'
Because amongst these are
Men devoted to learning
And men who have renounced the world,
and they are not arrogant."

Again, the Qur'an states (II:62):
"Those who believe (in the Qur'an)
And those who follow the Jewish Scriptures
And the Christians and the Sabians
And who believe in God
And the Last Day
And work righteously
Shall have their reward."

Abbas Hamdani is professor of Islamic History, University of Wisconsin at Milwaukee.

concept is held by many Christians. To Muslims, sin is the disobedience of responsible human beings to the law of Almighty God. It is caused by human weakness, by forgetfulness and by a spirit of rebellion.

Question: Is Islam fatalistic?

Answer: Not necessarily. The Qur'an describes a harmonious balance between the power of God and the free will of human beings. So the Qur'an is not fatalistic. True fatalism allows no place for the free will of the human. The fatalist refuses any personal responsibility for what happens, and says that fate, or God, is the only one responsible. In Islam, God is seen as the final source of all things. So, many observers have gained the impression that Muslims try to evade personal responsibility for their actions by attributing everything to God. However, such statements are made in times of human weakness and frustration. Normally, Muslims express just as much sense of personal involvement in life as do Christians.

Question: Do Muslims know about God's love?

Answer: In comparing concepts in Islam with those in Christianity, we must be careful not to restrict ourselves to words that seem to correspond exactly in English and in the Arabic of the Qur'an. For example, the Qur'an speaks about the love that God has for certain people and the love that he withholds from others. The Muslim Scripture says that God loves those who do good, the repentant and the pure, the pious, the patient ones, those who are trusting, and those who act with fairness. On the other hand, according to the Qur'an, God does not love the ungrateful or the oppressors. Obviously then, this word for "love" alone does not correspond to the Christian concept of God's love. This does not mean, however, that the corresponding idea is absent from Islam. It is found in the meanings of other words, one of the most significant being "mercy," as described in Chapter 4. Of course, "mercy" is not the exact equivalent of what is meant by *rahma* in Arabic. In some cases we could translate it by "love," that is, love as understood in Christian thought. The rahma of God is extended without distinction to all of creation, and those who respond to this universal rahma by faith and commitment become candidates for special rahma. So, we can say that Muslims know about God's love, although sometimes they use other words to express that thought. At the same time, it should be noted that Islam does not affirm that dimension of divine love that is central to Christian faith, that is, God's assuming the burden of human sin.

Question: Why do Muslims mix religion and state?

Answer: From their standpoint, they do not *mix* religion and state because these are not viewed as separate realms or entities. In Islam, religion is all-encompassing, so the activities of the state are simply one aspect of religion. Muslims believe that faith in God should affect the way the state is governed as much as it does the way prayers are said.

Question: Was Islam spread by the sword?

Answer: The political and economic control of Islamic governments was imposed by fighting as the Muslim armies spread

---

From Elliot and Trudy Bush, Delavan, Wisconsin

Participation in Milwaukee's Islamic-Christian Dialogue has not only given us the opportunity to learn more about Islam, it has enabled us to make Muslim friends. Our interest in Islam began fourteen years ago when we spent two years working in Algeria. We did a great deal of study of Islam at that time but, although Muslims were our colleagues, students and neighbors, the opportunities to share our faith as friends never developed. But in Milwaukee, meeting monthly for seven years with the same group of people, we have gotten to know and respect each other and have gained insight into the ways our faiths shape our lives and attitudes. Some of our best meetings have shared ways in which Islamic and Christian piety is expressed in daily life, or have explored how Muslims and Christians can work together on issues of common concern.

Another value of the dialogue is its ability to break down stereotypes. Hearing from Muslims on those issues where they agree with us, and where they differ from us, has opened our eyes to the variety of practices and attitudes within Islam. We hope that our Muslim friends have gained a similar perspective on Christianity.

A year ago, at the close of an exciting week of sharing with Muslims at a seminar sponsored by the National Council of Churches, it became clear to us that the greatest value of the dialogue is that it makes people of both faiths aware of their common values and aspirations: the desire for holiness, the quest for justice, and the love of peace. It is this that unites us in brotherhood and sisterhood and makes our dialogue group such an important part of our lives.

Elliot Bush is pastor of the United Methodist Church, Delavan.

their power across the ancient world. The misconception has prevailed among Western non-Muslims that those conquerors forced vast numbers of people to change their religion to that of Islam and killed those who refused to convert. Of course, excesses are committed in times of violent upheaval. War unleashes the worst of human passions. But careful study of the historical documents at our disposal indicates that the spread of Islamic faith in the hearts and lives of populations took place *after* the subjugation of the nations by the armies of Islam. The Muslim generals and governors were not interested in making converts among the peoples they conquered. So the old cliché that Islam was spread by the sword is untrue. After the initial invasions of their lands, thousands of Asians, Africans and Europeans became Muslims, but they were not forced to do so. It was the general voluntary attachment to the Islamic way of life and to the Qur'an that held the vast domain of Islam together over the centuries. Politically, this realm broke up fairly quickly into many kingdoms and princedoms, but the umma of Islam, discussed in Chapter 4, was always a transcending reality, drawing peoples who were otherwise widely divergent into a sense of unity under God.

Question: Does the Golden Rule exist in Islam?

Answer: Although it is not called by that name, an exhortation from the Prophet conveys the same meaning as the "Golden Rule." It is found in the collection of hadith texts, or traditions of the Prophet, compiled by Al-Bukhari. It says, "You are not really believers if you do not desire for your fellow Muslims that which you desire for yourself" (*Al-Jami' al-Sahih*, Book of Faith, Chapter 7).

Question: What if we listen respectfully to Muslims, trying to be conciliatory toward them, and then they do not listen respectfully to us or try to be conciliatory toward us?

Answer: Obviously, it takes two parties for there to be reconciliation and mutual understanding. The process is blocked if only one party makes the friendly approach. If there is not a mutual, two-way interaction at first, we have to be patient. The lack of response on the Muslim side may be due to any of several factors that we have been discussing in this book. In such cases, we simply renew our initiatives of peaceful approach and remain ready to repeat them until cooperation is achieved.

6

Our Common Situation
As Muslims and Christians

*U*p to now the description of Islam has concentrated on those elements that differ from Christianity: words, rites, emphases, structures, laws, ways of thinking. This final chapter will deal with common ground shared by Islam and Christianity. Here we are looking at similarities. I hope that by now readers will feel enough grace and friendliness for Muslims to be able to accept these similarities with gratitude and joy, at least those elements that seem favorable to both religions. It we are alike in less favorable ways as well, then learning about them should help us to express solidarity with those of the other religion and to share the burden of responsibility.

The things we Muslims and Christians hold in common should draw us together. For centuries our forebears concentrated on differences between the two faiths in order to attack Islam, and Muslims did the same toward Christianity. The only result was alienation and animosity. It is time to capitalize on our similarities, not in a naive way that glosses over disagreements, but in a generous way that seeks to go as far as possible on the strength of common ground.

Beliefs

The centrality and reality of the one true and living God is the basic rallying point for Christians and Muslims. Living daily as conscious and grateful recipients of the gifts of an Almighty and Gracious Creator, we have a scope for mutual understanding as broad as any human experience. What is more, we talk about God with many of the same words: Just, True, Beneficent, Wise, Powerful, Loving, Holy, Exalted, All-Hearing, All-Knowing.

We both believe in prophets who were God's instruments in human history to draw men and women from unbelief into the life of faith. History is taken seriously by our two religions, since both faiths are founded on concrete historical events.

The place of Jesus differs enormously in the Muslim and the Christian systems, but the fact that he is known and respected in both is an important point of meeting.

We both believe that our deeds in life have importance for the present and for the future, because the world is hastening toward the day of resurrection and judgment, when justice will finally be realized, good rewarded and evil punished.

Not only is our outlook essentially similar as we try to make the world a better place, but the principles that guide our actions are similar. In an earlier chapter, the moral standards of Islam were examined, and they were found to be much like ours.

Both faiths invite their believers to a life of prayer and worship, in grateful and dutiful response to the goodness of God. Prayer is the basic activity of Christians and Muslims. Their religious experience offers them the privilege and duty of sustained, conscious and structured communication with God. Believers have described in several ways what moves them to pray. In general, Christians have emphasized that even as earthly children talk readily with their parents, so believers should, as spiritual children, address the Living God in freedom and respect, through prayer. Muslims see prayer as a principal way to manifest outwardly their inner determination to obey the divine will as well as the humility of spirit that befits the creatures of God. Prayer is, for Muslims, an act of homage, and a way to combat any inclination toward evil. Christians would certainly agree with these Islamic reasons for praying.

Muslims and Christians are people with Scriptures, even though their holy Books are different. The scriptural foundation of faith and practice makes possible a very great degree of mutual understanding.

Both religions are universal in perspective, offered to all of humankind as the key to fullness of life. Even though this similarity helps Muslims and Christians understand each other, it is also the source of considerable tension: how should we understand the existence of two universal religions in one world?

Believers

As might be expected, given the general consistency of human nature across cultures and generations, Christians and Muslims demonstrate a variety of common responses to their respective religions.* In both communities most followers are simple believers who worship more or less regularly but show only a modest grasp of the teachings of their faith. They have strong emotional attachments to their religious community, but their lack of education in religion makes them susceptible to superstitious ideas. In the solidly Islamic countries, such believers are at home in what Muslims call "The Abode of Islam." Other countries still have populations that are solidly Christian. These lands, of which Spain and some Latin American countries are examples, are the only remaining areas that can be called "Christendom." By and large, however, the masses of Christians no longer find themselves "at home" in homogeneous populations. They, together with increasing numbers of Muslims, are sharing life with people of other religions or of no religion. The breakup of the secure and familiar spiritual environment in which large numbers of uninstructed believers live is a challenge to faith for both religions.

At another level, both faith communities have some traditional believers who have received religious educations. These tend to be the conservatives, the bastion of the old-fashioned ways of doing things, who do not follow tradition blindly but know their Scriptures and law books and consider themselves to be the protectors of the faith. They are the ones who seek to arouse the less-informed to greater faithfulness in practice and who try to educate youth in the tenets of the religion. In the churches, these are the people who assume the greatest responsibility for maintaining religious activities.

The next group I call the modernists, for want of a better word. In both religions they form a minority, but an articulate, active and influential minority. They are often highly educated and sympathetic to innovative ideas, both in theology and in practice. Denominational agencies, theological seminaries and universities, along with ecumenical agencies, provide the Christians of this outlook with a forum in which to operate. In Islam they have no forum as yet, but must write, speak and act independently.

I am not suggesting an additional category of socially active believers as being common to both Islam and Christianity. Among Christians a distinction between social activists and

---

* In the following paragraphs about different categories of believers, I am indebted to the suggestive remarks by Maurice Boormans in *Orientations pour un dialogue entre chretiens et musulmans* (Paris: Le Cerf, 1981).

others certainly exists, but in Islam social action is so integral a part of the faith structure that such a distinction can seldom be drawn.

As a final group that is common to both religions, we recognize what might be called the resurgents. The mass media like to use "fundamentalists" to describe these believers, whether in Christianity or in Islam. But the word is emotionally charged, and is quite inaccurate when applied to the whole category of what I am calling resurgents. Resurgents can come either from the group of traditionally trained believers or from the modernists, but all have adopted a "back-to-basics" ideology that has galvanized them into action and set them apart from their less

---

Muslims in the Americas: New Mexico

What would it mean to have a community in North America whose members could live a fully Islamic way of life? Dar al-Islam, the Abode of the Faithful, a community being built on a former ranch near Abiquiu, New Mexico, is the culmination of a dream—a place where American Muslims can engage in life's daily transactions according to their beliefs in the *deen*, or code of Islam and thus bear the witness of Islam to others, which is the *da'wa*, or calling.

Incorporated in 1980 as a non-profit religious and educational foundation, Dar al-Islam is the first Islamic village in the U.S. Planned as the eventual home of 150 families, it is home already to more than 30. The adult American-born among them have come to Islam from sister monotheistic traditions, Christian and Jewish, or in some cases from agnosticism. The community has also welcomed a number of Muslims from Canada, Ireland, Holland and Belgium, from Turkey, Syria, Jordan and Iraq.

When Abdullah Nuridin Durkee, the director of the foundation, and his wife, Nura, were studying Arabic and Islamic law in Mecca in the late 1970s, they met Saudi Arabians who encouraged them to realize the dream of an Islamic community in the U.S. Today the foundation is supported by individual Muslims in the Middle East and the U.S. and by some small private businesses that community members have established near the village.

The foundation supervises three areas: the mosque and school; lands and housing; and an Institute of Traditional Islamic Studies. The adobe mosque was designed by Egyptian architect Hassan Fathy. A connecting school has been mostly completed. In 1986-87, 44 children were enrolled in the school, which teaches standard

activist sisters and brothers. The story of Christian resurgence is well-known, whether the stances of these activists identify them as being on the right wing or the left. Liberation theology, prayer and religion in the public schools, rights of women, questions of sexual and medical ethics, nuclear strategy, pornography, war and peace—these are some of the issues that preoccupy Christian resurgents. In Islam the most well-known resurgents are the groups of militants who carried out the Iranian Revolution and who disturb the status quo in a number of other Muslim countries. These groups have been so prominent in the news recently that it is fitting to provide some background for an understanding of their activities.

school subjects along with a solid grounding in Islamic values as well as classes in Arabic and the Qur'an. The Institute holds a variety of programs and seminars for teachers in Muslim schools and others who want to learn about Islam in an Islamic setting.

Dar al-Islam provides a special place where worship and education, daily relationships with family and neighbors, business, eating and all of life's transactions can take place in faithfulness. But community members do not see themselves as isolated. They are part of the worldwide community of Islam. And they are connected in special ways to mainstream America. Local people are hired to work alongside Dar al-Islam's Muslims; Muslims patronize Abiquiu businesses and rent houses in the village. The foundation contributes to the local fire department and the local Head Start program. Students from surrounding areas and visitors from across the nation drive up the dirt road to admire the adobe mosque above the Chama River and think about why it is there. Many record their thoughts in the guest books, whose pages are filled with words such as "serene" and "spiritual."

Adapted from "Dar al-Islam: The Code and the Calling," by William Tracy. Photo by William Tracy. Courtesy of *Aramco World*, May-June 1988.

Islamic Resurgence in the Modern World

The mass media speak often of Islamic renewal. News comes of the resurgence of Islam in several countries, about militant Muslims, a religion on the march, Islamic peoples who are asserting themselves in disturbing ways, and countries such as Iran and Pakistan that affirm their public policies in terms of their religious faith. Such reports deeply interest and puzzle American Christians. The United States is involved in the movement of Islamic peoples, in the sense that some Muslims see the U.S. as their enemy and others look to Americans for support in asserting their Islamic identity. Like Christian resurgents, Islamic resurgents are openly bringing God and their faith into public life. Their ideal is to affirm the sovereignty of God over political life and the validity of the shari'a for all times. This goal strikes some Americans as novel and upsetting because the American tradition of separating church from state has conditioned them against bringing religion into public life. In reality, most Christians acknowledge that their God reigns over the marketplace and the legislature as well as in individual lives. The resurgents from both communities are reminding us of the connection between religion and politico-economic life.

Many Americans have been surprised by the prominent place on the world scene occupied by countries that are predominantly Muslim during the last few years. Until now, the USA has managed to live without paying much attention to those lands, whereas Canada has shown more awareness of them. The U.S. has not lived completely without them, though, because it has used the lands of Islam as markets for its manufactured goods, its agricultural products and its technology. Some of those nations have provided the petroleum with which Americans run their machines and heat their homes. The USA has considered the countries of Islam as arenas in which to strive for advantage over the USSR. And one of the predominantly Islamic lands was used to provide a national home for the Jews. In 1948, together with its allies, the USA promoted the creation of the state of Israel to serve as a haven for the much-persecuted Jews. The only difficulty was that in so doing, the Western powers became guilty of the injustice of ignoring the desires of the Palestinian people, Muslims and Christians, who already lived on the land that became Israel.

So, while Americans were living almost as though the Muslim nations did not exist, they were reaping benefit from them. In return, the benefit the Muslims received—access to Western goods and cultural practices—was, to them, hardly worth the cost. The U.S. was and is considered as an aggressor by many in the lands of Islam. We need to understand this perspective in order to grasp the meaning of the resurgence of Islam in the modern world. The United States was only one in a group of countries that followed patterns of injustice in dealing with Muslim countries. France, England, Holland and Italy actually conquered and colonized those predominantly Muslim areas. The USSR absorbed millions of Muslims and their homelands into its sphere of control. Americans were not colonialists, strictly speaking, but they imposed their particular political and economic interests upon the peoples of Islam in an imperious fashion. Because of America's strength as a world power since World War II, Muslims focus much of their antagonism on the U.S.

These days, several of the Islamic states are reacting strongly to the injustices of the past. They are trying to define their relation to the modern world on their own terms, not simply as the tools of stronger powers. Expressed in this way, as an affirmation of identity and will, and as resistance to oppression, there is nothing specifically Islamic about the resurgence. For example, Israel, which is considered in the Middle East to be an instrument of the imperialist Americans, is opposed by Christian Arabs as well as by Muslim Arabs. The conflict over Israel does not set one religion (Islam) against another (Judaism), but one ethnic and political group against another.

Technology, the scientific know-how that plays such an important part in the resurgence of the countries under consideration, is also religiously neutral. Technology itself is not Muslim or Christian. The resurgence is not, then, a religious opposition to a nation established by members of another religion, nor is it the quest to obtain or reject the tools of universal technological civilization. But neither is the resurgence simply a revival of religious fervor. Religious fervor has always existed in Islam. A few authoritarian and alien regimes tried to suppress it. Earlier in this century, for example, Kemal Ataturk in Turkey and France in colonial Algeria tried to isolate religion from the mainstream of life in order to render it innocuous. These rulers discovered that Muslim piety is an abiding force. The inclusive system of Islam penetrates to every cell of the corporate life of a people. As the fortunes of nations have risen and fallen through the years, millions of Muslims have remained passionately devoted to the Qur'an and to the example of the Prophet.

Properly speaking, the resurgence of Islam is not just a revival of religious feeling but a reaffirmation of Islamic identity, a renewed effort to collect and to concentrate the scattered forces of Islamic civilization, to bring into order that which is in disarray. In a word, it seeks to focus again the intellectual, economic, political and social resources of Muslim people on living authentically as believers in the modern world.

Many factors have converged to make the present a time of Islamic resurgence. Briefly, we can point out that during the nineteenth century, even while the colonial powers held sway, a modest cultural renewal got under way, especially in the Arab world and in India, involving both Muslims and other religious groups. Then, in the twentieth century, peoples in many places of the world initiated a protracted struggle for political and economic independence. As the various Islamic peoples, freed from imperial control, joined the world family of nations, some of them went through a short-lived experiment with secular ideologies, either in imitation of their former colonial rulers or in an effort to gain technical competence and economic viability

---

Religious Roadblocks in a Secular Society

The early [Muslim] immigrants [to the United States] faced grave problems in establishing Islam. Mostly uneducated and unacquainted with American bureaucracy, they felt discrimination in their jobs as well as in their efforts to erect houses of prayer. Zoning laws obstructed them. They found themselves unable to teach Islam to their children for want of materials in English....

It is almost impossible for Muslims to fulfill the duty of praying five times a day at prescribed times, including noon and early afternoon, without facing ridicule or pressure from their peers. The author is aware of one Muslim who lost his job because he was performing ablutions (the ritual cleansing necessary before prayer of such parts of the body as the hands, feet, elbows, ears, face and head) in the men's room. Prayer also necessitates a clean area with no pictures or portraits hanging on the walls.

Muslims are expected to join other believers in the communal prayer on Friday, an impossibility for many.... All mosques hold Sunday services, which are only alternative meetings and do not replace the efficacy of Friday worship.

The two most important holidays of Islam, 'Id al-Fitr (celebrated at the end of the month of fasting) and 'Id al-Adha (observed by

quickly. But the newly formed Islamic nations grew disillusioned with such a course relatively soon. They saw the structure of faith as a better way to undergird national life. Finally, the economic power created by gaining control over the oil resources of their lands probably triggered the more or less sudden Muslim resurgence that is in progress.

To summarize, Islam is what it has always been: a way of life based upon faith in the living, creator God. By the fortunes of history, the people of Muslim areas have lived for many centuries with little development in technology according to Western models. This lack of development left them vulnerable to powerful forces in the West that took advantage of them. Now they have some power of their own, and they are reacting aggressively, drawing inspiration from their Islamic faith. Taken aback by the vehemence of this resurgence, Americans often have fallen back on their prejudices and misinformation about Islam and have put the worst possible interpretation on events that have been but imperfectly reported.

The Islamic resurgence is not a uniform phenomenon. In some areas, "back-to-basics" militants have the upper hand. In

Muslims worldwide at the end of the hajj ...) are not recognized holidays in this country. Muslim students are not excused from classes, nor are workers given a day off to participate in these celebrations. *(con't. next page)*

People of several faiths learn about the Islamic Center in Washington, D.C., on a visit organized by the Interfaith Conference of Metropolitan Washington. Photo by Morton Broffman.

other places, modern-thinking technocrats, who are also loyal believers, direct national policy. In still other cases, political power blocs hold sway by soliciting the support of a religious elite who are interested in maintaining the status quo. In these last situations, Islamic resurgence is of minimal strength. In Iran, Muslims brought forth an Islamic Revolution that began in opposition to the secularizing measures of the late Shah. In Egypt, resurgence can be seen at the levels both of the moderate regime in power and of the radical underground. The latter expresses people's disillusionment with their government's slow process of modernization, dismay at the invasion of alien moral values, and vexation at the elusiveness of a comprehensive settlement with Israel.

Syrian Muslim revolutionaries are angry at their government's secular policies and its friendship with the Russians.

In Indonesia, where the vast majority of the huge population is Muslim, the resurgent elements feel that Islam has been the victim of discriminatory governmental policies.

These examples emphasize the variety of circumstances in which the Islamic resurgence is taking place.

Religious Roadblocks, continued

The practice of Islam in the United States is hampered by American civil laws which are different from Islamic laws governing divorce, alimony, child custody and support, marriage, inheritance and adoption. Islamic law is derived from the teachings of the Qur'an, which define God's ways for mankind. Thus, by living in America and adhering to American law, the Muslim may be forced to accept judgments that contradict the will of God.

Muslims often see overindulgent American culture based on materialism as going against the Islamic ethos. The Qur'an teaches that [the human creature] was placed on the earth to administer it for God. The emphasis on consumption and planned obsolescence is paramount to mismanagement of resources; the goals of individualism and personal gratification jeopardize the Muslim teaching of corporate commitment and responsibility. Individual satisfaction leads to exclusiveness and discrimination which are contrary to the revelation of the Qur'an affirming that all people are brothers and sisters. The only way one human being can excel over another is in piety and devotion to God.

From "The Muslim Experience in North America," by Yvonne Y. Haddad. From Sept./Oct. 1979 issue of "The Link," published by Americans for Middle East Understanding; used by permission.

Because of Islam's egalitarian nature, the various resurgent societies are not likely to unite under a single worldwide, or even region-wide, authority. But some Muslim groups are concerned to develop concrete expressions of worldwide Islamic solidarity. Organizations such as the Islamic Conference, the Development Bank, the Muslim World League and the Islamic Da'wa (Mission Agency) are examples of a new kind of international cooperation.

Polarities Cause Tensions

We have looked at some patterns of response to faith that can characterize both Christian and Muslim believers. Another kind of pattern emerges if we examine some tensions generated within each faith community when individuals or groups emphasize some belief or practice they consider essential to faith. Some of these areas of tension that arise within Islam have many parallells to areas of tension that arise within Christianity, and vice versa. Here are some of the areas in which Christians and Muslims may recognize similar attitudes, debates, tensions

---

Dietary Requirements for Muslims

Keeping the dietary restrictions in Islam requires extra care in food selection for Muslims in pluralistic societies like Canada and the U.S. These restrictions will remind readers of the kind of regulations that exists in Judaism, although the two codes are not identical. The Qur'an gives the basic rules for Muslims:

O believers, eat of the good things that we have provided for you and give thanks to God, if it is indeed he whom you worship. He has forbidden you to eat carrion, blood and the meat of swine, as well as the flesh of any animal not slaughtered in the name of God. But if necessity requires it no sin is committed by those who eat what is forbidden, provided they eat with restraint. (Sura "The Cow," No. 2, vs. 172, 173)

　O believers, liquor, games of chance, idols and divination are works of Satan. (Sura "The Table Spread," No. 5, v. 90)

Islamic law provides many details of dietary requirements based upon interpretations and applications of these verses. For example, the prohibition of wine is held to include drugs and tobacco. And, in a general way, the flesh of all animals that are repugnant to humans, such as serpents, rats and scorpions, is forbidden to Muslims. *RMS*

and polarities. On the Christian side I shall only mention the area, assuming that most readers are reasonably familiar with Christian ways of thinking.

1. Emphasis on predestination in contrast to emphasis on human free will. Some of the greatest debates in Islamic theology argued this subject. The questions asked and answers proposed are remarkably parallel to those asked and proposed in Christian theology. Both Muslim and Christian Scriptures hold God's sovereign will in beautiful balance with human choice, without confusing the two ideas. But in each religion theologians who have tried to reconcile these two great truths by using logic have met with little success. Ordinary believers often tend to emphasize one side of the balance or the other. Although open theological debate about free will and predestination is out-of-date in both religions, tension between the two truths still affects religious people everywhere. When believers seek to make responsible decisions in accord with the divine will or to understand the ways God works in the world, they can experience this tension.

2. Unquestioning obedience to religious and scriptural traditions in contrast to reliance on God-given intelligence in deciding questions of ethics and ritual. This tension once caused history-making debates between Islamic experts because Muslims emphasize correct practice so much. Among Christians today this polarity comes very much to the fore in arguments about moral standards, social ethics and authority. Of course modern Muslims are also affected by these issues.

3. Faith in contrast to works. No question in Islam or in Christianity has had a more far-reaching effect than the definition of faith and its relationship to human deeds. Are works a part of faith, or completely distinct from it? Is faith alone sufficient for a right standing with God? The two religions are not the same in their use and understanding of "salvation," but when discussing faith and works, they are so much alike that some of the Muslim arguments on the side of faith could be used by Christians on the same side, and vice versa.

4. Austerity in contrast to seeking pleasure in the created world. This contrast is more marked in Christianity, with its strong tradition of asceticism (strict self-denial), than in Islam; but among Muslims some have stressed a tendency to severe self-discipline as opposed to those who are more accepting of worldly pleasures.

5. Religious authority located in a structured system of lead-

ership in contrast to religious authority located in the equal participation of all believers. The contrast between the Shi'a (described in Chapter 4) and the Sunnis in regard to the structure of authority finds one Christian parallel in the difference between episcopal and congregational forms of church government.

6. Educated religious practice in contrast to popular practices. Training in practices of worship and in doctrine sets a minority in both faiths apart from the majority, whose beliefs and worship are often affected by cultural factors that do not belong to strictly scriptural and legal traditions. The term "folk religion" is often used to describe the beliefs and practices of those who are uninstructed in their faith.

7. Conservatives as opposed to liberals. These terms are overly general, but their broad meaning is fairly clear: the tension between those who want to keep things as they have always been and those who are open to change, even drastic change. In Islamic countries the two tendencies do not characterize political parties so much as they mark divisions within groups of scholars and technocrats in whose hands lies the socio-economic future of their nations. Loyalty to Islam binds such groups together, but their liberal or conservative convictions regarding the goals of their societies keep them widely separated.

Modern Challenges to Faith

So far, in thinking about the common situation of Muslims and Christians we have dwelt on the ways in which we understand and express our religious identity. In view of the remarkable concordance between our two communities at so many levels, it seems all the more appropriate for us to learn to know each other's faiths better, to encourage ongoing consultations from local to worldwide levels and to be on friendly terms as individuals.

Still another aspect of our common situation, and one of dramatic importance, is that we both face the multiple challenges to our faith posed by standards and conditions of present-day society. Such difficulties and threats to faith are often set before Christians by press and pulpit. When I mention a few details of these challenges as Muslims perceive them, those from the Christian community will easily resonate to the concerns.

1. The crisis of religious practice. Only a minority of the

Muslim community in many places is faithful in praying five times a day, giving zakat and participating in communal worship. In factories, schools, airports, banks and other modern work situations, the atmosphere is simply not conducive to moments of worship.

2. Linked with the crisis of religious practice is the challenge of continuing secularization (especially in Western countries), whereby religion is compartmentalized and reduced to a subsidiary activity alongside other, more "serious" activities: making a living or getting an education. Of course a secular outlook on life threatens the whole Islamic way. Effects of secularization are seen especially among young people, raising questions about the goals of education.

3. The overwhelming impact of the mass media, especially television, on life. Audiovisual communication is still a valuable tool for mass education in many developing countries of the Islamic world, but where advertizing and light entertainment monopolize the media, Muslims are apprehensive.

4. Inequitable distribution of wealth. The glaring gap between rich and poor in societies where the quest for gain has become a supreme value is viewed with alarm by many Muslims. They recognize that some Islamic countries have failed to live up to the shari'a in this regard, and one effort of the resurgents is to right that wrong. In North American and other pluralistic societies, concerted efforts are being made to inculcate Islamic economic ideals among the faithful.

5. The threat of nuclear war. Many Muslims see the possession of nuclear weapons by great powers as another kind of imperialism. By keeping atomic weapons away from other countries, members of the "nuclear club" can hold non-nuclear nations in effective subjugation.

6. Nationalism. Muslims were drawn into the modern ideology of nationalism as a result of the breakup of colonial empires in this century. Many see nationalism as a serious threat to the universal perspective of the Islamic umma.

7. The emancipation of women. Conservatives fear the worst as Western ideas of women's liberation spread across the world and as Muslim women begin to assume new roles in society. Others are responding with a sharp counter-challenge, presenting the Islamic alternative as a positive, enriching choice for women. They say that only in Islam, rightly understood and practiced, can women find the fulfillment, security, justice and respect that they deserve. Middle Eastern women have been

articulate in trying to counteract Western secular influences. Many Muslims see aspects of women's liberation as directly related to the weakening of the traditional family structure in Western countries.

The fact that Muslims have presented an alternative to women's emancipation as carried out in the West makes us aware that besides experiencing many situations in common, Christians and Muslims also conduct their lives in particular local circumstances that are markedly different. At no point are these differences more apparent than when the question of women's rights is raised.

Most Western readers of this book are living in the full light of advancing liberation of women from past injustices and prejudice. Over the past century and a half, women in many countries have worked to change their roles in society, to be

---

Women in Islamic Spiritual Tradition

In the later part of the eighth century, the woman mystic Rabia al-Adawiyya (died 801) introduced the element of pure love into Sufi expression. Divine love became the means by which the seeker was empowered with the capacity to bear the affliction that God visits on the ascetic to test his intent and purify his soul. Divine love is the agent that transforms asceticism into true mysticism. Through its mediation, the Sufi attains insight and knowledge of divine mysteries. The fact that a woman played an important role at the very beginning of Sufi history seems typical. Throughout the ages we find names of pious women who pursued the mystical path, either independently or as consorts or mothers of Sufis. Many of their names are noted in the hagiographical works, and the memory of many saintly women is kept alive in small sanctuaries found in North Africa, Anatolia, and particularly in Muslim India. (These sanctuaries are not accessible to men.) This role of women is not astonishing since in the Islamic Middle Ages women participated in various aspects of social life. We know of not only poetesses and calligraphers but also a considerable number of transmitters of the traditions of the Prophet and even ruling princesses such as Shajarat al-Durr in Egypt (died 1249) or Raziya Sultana of Delhi (reigned 1236-1240). In the mystical life, women have played an important role to this day; even some successful leaders in the modern traditions have been women.

From "Aspects of Mystical Thought in Islam" by Annemarie Schimmel in *The Islamic Impact*, edited by Haddad, Haines and Findly (Syracuse; Syracuse University Press, 1984). Used by permission.

acknowledged as equal partners in marriage and as equal citizens in the public realm, including the world of work. This movement has involved Christians in much new theological and biblical interpretation. In the last few decades, Christian "resurgents" have argued both for and against the redefinitions of women's social roles and the reformulation of some Christian beliefs.

When those Christians and others who value women's equality in faith and society observe the situation in predominantly Muslim lands, especially in areas where Islamic resurgence is in progress, they may wonder if Muslim women are not being subjected to redoubled injustice. Western media report how women in Iran and Egypt, for example, dress in the veil more often than before, and how women's rights are denied in several areas of life. Westerners who have only media reports to go by ask themselves if Muslim women are not victims of the recent Islamic resurgence (a movement that also has been growing for a century or more).

Some Muslim women do object strongly to the traditional role of women in their societies. These are women who have found their own identity and freedom shaped by exposure to secular ways of thinking and living. A few have turned to a scholarly search of Islamic traditions, finding affirmations of women's positive role that they believe have been neglected in their societies.

These are also the women whose voices we in the West are most likely to hear. Their voice is authentic, but it is only one voice. Their view of the situation is a minority view, one colored by their experiences of the mingling of cultures—often a painful, conflictual mingling. As sympathetic friends of Muslims, we must try to hear all sides of the issues. Our judgments about the status and conditions of women in Islam will not be adequate until we hear from many Muslim women. To do so may take a long time and will stretch our listening skills, because the environments from which they and we speak, think and react are very different. And it is exactly these different environments that influence our judgments about what is desirable and good in life.

Conclusion: Adversaries or Parallel Witnesses?

Until now the two religious communities of Islam and Christianity have maintained their distance even in countries where

Praising God, Learning from One Another

Shaikh Fathy Mady, Mu'adhin at the Islamic Center of Washington, D.C., recites from the Qur'an during the 1988 Interfaith Choral Concert at the National Shrine of the Immaculate Conception in Washington. The passage he recited was from Sura 59, vss. 18-24, emphasizing the oneness of God.

The concert was the ninth sponsored by the Interfaith Conference of Metropolitan Washington (IFC). At present, 29 judicatories, associations and religious organizations of the Jewish, Islamic, Sikh, Mormon, Protestant and Roman Catholic faiths are conference members. The conference logo (*below*) represents one source of unity: all members hold scripture as central to their faiths.

Each year the IFC also sponsors occasions for interfaith dialogue and assists local congregations in similar ventures. The IFC gathers religious leaders to reflect and act on community and public concerns in the metropolitan Washington area, presses for needed changes in public policy, and helps form coalitions that can meet the concerns. Not itself a direct service agency, it is supportive of various community agencies and each fall publishes an Emergency Food and Shelter Directory for the Washington area. The Rev. Clark Lobenstine is Executive Director of IFC. (Photo by Carl V. Hylton).

both make up large elements of the population. In one sense, for communities to follow their separate ways is only natural, because each needed the sense of unity and cohesion around its beliefs and practices in order to maintain its particular religious identity. To mingle closely with each other might have weakened this sense of uniqueness. However, the practice of keeping our distances led to several unhappy results through the years. Gulfs of ignorance about each other have never been bridged. In spite of the many things said in the Qur'an about Christ and Christianity, Muslims still do not generally have a practical

---

Another Model of Cooperation

Since 1979, Presbyterians in Detroit have been involved in a program committed to building bridges of understanding between the Muslim and Christian communities and beyond. Recognizing that Detroit is home to about 200,000 persons of Middle Eastern background, and that their own community included nearly 20,000 Arabic-speaking persons, of whom 90 percent are Muslims, the Littlefield Presbyterian Church in Dearborn began the American Arab Ministry program. Now a ministry of the Presbytery of Detroit, the program combines a three-fold outreach.

1. It works to extend awareness of the American Arab community, of other faiths, especially Islam, and of the Middle East to local churches and community groups and to its denomination. People in the program listen closely to Arab-American concerns into order to help speak for these concerns to local school, community, government and other organizations.

2. In cooperation with community service groups, especially the Arab Community Center for Economic and Social Services, the ministry shows neighborly concern for local Arab Americans. In particular, it has been helpful to people who are new to the community and the country, assisting with immigration procedures and offering English language classes. Some emergency assistance is provided to families and students as well as some pastoral services to local Arab Christians.

3. The ministry promotes interfaith discussion and understanding, helping to arrange meetings between Christians, Muslims and Jews, and sponsoring seminars, community activities, and services of worship.

Based on information supplied by the Rev. William Gepford, director of the American Arab Ministry. On page 131 is a statement of the ministry's vision for its future, adapted from the Islamic Study Advisory Committee's report to the General Assembly, Presbyterian Church (USA), 1987.

knowledge of why Christians think and act as they do. To a great extent, Muslims have lived as if Christians existed only as a phenomenon of past history or as a present force to be opposed. Likewise, through the centuries Christians have led their lives apart from Muslims, with only the vaguest notions of who they are and what they stand for. Then when tumult involving Islamic peoples has arisen—the oil crisis in the Middle East and the Iranian Revolution, for example—Christians have not had enough knowledge to be able to interpret these occurrences accurately. So, their separation from Muslims, taken for granted for so long, has been accentuated, leading to further alienation.

Many religious people believe that it is their task to disseminate their faith in the world; this concern is especially vital to both Muslims and Christians, who belong to missionary religions. Living apart from each other, two groups of believers almost inevitably developed a sense of being adversaries as each sought to spread its religion in the world. Even today, many Christians, especially those with keen missionary motivation, feel that Islam and Christianity are engaged in a spiritual contest to win the souls of people everywhere. These Christians consider Islam to be a major hindrance to the worldwide spread of Christianity. From their side, Muslims look on countries that have traditionally been Christian as having failed to fulfill the moral and spiritual needs of their people. They hold Islam up as the solution to humanity's anguish.

Looking Ahead: New Understanding, New Grace

The American Arab Ministry looks toward its future; from the ministry's report to the Presbytery of Detroit, October 1988:

Islamic religious renewal has released immense spiritual and emotional forces within the Muslim/Arab community. The response of Christians to this phenomenon must be one of discernment, realism and faith in the sovereignty of God over the world. In this one area of Christian-Muslim relations particularly, the search for faithful witness must be motivated by a desire to love God, to be obedient to God's will and to love neighbors as ourselves. Where this may lead and how it will bring new understanding and cooperation among Christians and Muslims, and Christians and Jews, rests in the mercy and grace of God. Christians are challenged to allow God, as revealed through Jesus Christ, to guide them into a future free of hatred, free of fear and directed by hopeful love.

the purposes of this book is to help Christians look
vithout perceiving Muslims as adversaries. To me, the
opposition between religions has a cheap and super-
 If the question were of a conflict between evil and
righteousness, then one religion might be justified in taking
sides against the other. Or if the issue were absolute truth versus
error, then talking about antagonism might make sense. But
when we learn that both Islam and Christianity come out
strongly on the side of righteousness, then how can they oppose
each other? And when both Muslims and Christians affirm in
common certain basic truths about divine revelation, how can
they be adversaries? Of course, each religion feels that its version
of truth is the accurate one; the two faiths will always be in
discussion about their varying doctrines. But unless we insist
that everyone think and believe exactly the way we do, it does
not make sense to set ourselves over against each other as
adversaries in a so-called spiritual war for the souls of human
beings.

In summary, let us recall some basic truths about divine
revelation that Christians and Muslims hold in common.

*1. There is only one God, almighty and all-merciful,
creator of all things and sustainer of life.*

*2. When human beings learn of God's power and mercy,
or grace, they must respond in a three-fold way, by
   a. a life of commitment to the divine will and
authority;
   b. a life of gratitude for the gifts of God; and
   c. a life of responsible action, in worship, charity and
acts of righteousness.*

*3. Life's choices are full of significance, because there
will be a final reckoning when all people must give an
account of the deeds they have done. Justice will be
finally realized.*

Neither Muslims nor Christians will be satisfied with the
stark reduction of beliefs to such brief sentences. For one thing,
Christians base their distinctiveness on the belief that Jesus the
Christ spells out with infinite richness *how* God is gracious to
humankind. And Muslims would affirm their conviction that
God has made explicit the kind of life required of believers by
revealing the shari'a, or holy law. It is in elaborating upon the
three points above and many others that each religion expresses
its distinctiveness. Calling attention in such an elemental way to

common beliefs does not in any way minimize the uniqueness of each faith. But it does emphasize the fact that we cannot with justice be considered as antagonistic religions. If we are both bearing witness to the same basic truths, then we Muslims and Christians are parallel witnesses rather than opposing witnesses. So it would be better for us to concentrate on understanding, respect for each other, reconciliation between us and cooperation in as many ways as possible.

There is a text in the Qur'an that illustrates the folly of hostility in theology and mission. God is said to have spoken thus to Jews, Christians and Muslims:

> *We have revealed Scripture to you with truth, confirming and safeguarding previously revealed Scriptures. . . . To each one [of the religious communities] we have given a law and a way. If God had willed he would have made all of you one community. But, that which you have has been given you so that he might test you thereby. Outdo one another, then, in good deeds, turning, all of you, toward God your goal. Finally he will let you know how you differed from each other.* (Sura 5, "The Table," verse 48)

This text teaches that God's sovereign power could have created all people to be of one religion, but that the divine wisdom saw that a diversity of religions would serve humankind better than doctrinal uniformity. Believers are told that, since the question of ultimate truth is not at stake in a religiously plural world (". . . turning all of you, toward God your goal"), they should concentrate on making their way toward God together while engaged in only one kind of contest, out of which all will emerge winners, a sublime sort of rivalry in good deeds. The image of "vying with one another in good deeds" recurs several times in the Qur'an as a theme that transforms the mundane human motive of competition into a stimulus for the highest and best moral behavior.

Although many Christians would hesitate to accept this Muslim explanation for the existence of many religions in the world, they may find the idea of "rivalry in good deeds" fruitful for thought. For although the image of Christians vying with one other, even in a figurative way, is almost absent from the New Testament, yet in his letter to the Romans, the Apostle Paul wrote, "Be kindly affectioned one to another with brotherly love, in honor preferring one another" (Romans 12:10, King James

Version). The Revised Standard Version renders the second part of the exhortation as, "Outdo one another in showing honor." This translation comes close to the thought of competition in good deeds, specifically, the deed of giving honor to one's neighbor.

In his book on Romans, Karl Barth shows how Christians can practice this principle without falling into the often hypocritical politeness of paying compliments to one another in a merely ceremonial way. People who do that, he says, are only honoring themselves, even though they pretend to be honoring others. To be a truly moral action, the respect Paul calls Christians to show "must be an unconditional, genuine preference, which expects nothing in return" (Barth).

Of course Paul did not have people of another religion in mind when he wrote thus to the Roman Christians. But we, having examined some of the close similarities between the Muslims and ourselves—some of the things that draw us together in our common situation of burden and mystery—can see that the principle of "outdoing one another" in goodness is a reliable guide for action in our life together. We can join Muslims in a "contest" of good works, since, as we compete it is always in esteem for them, showing sincere honor to them and to their works of righteousness. In this way we can be saved from the strife of religious antagonism.

**A Prayer of
Thankful Praise**

Great was thy light
   and Thou didst guide us:
Praise be to Thee!
Great was thy clemency
   and Thou didst pardon us:
Praise be to Thee!
Thou didst extend Thy hand
   and give to us:
Praise be to Thee!

A prayer of the Prophet according to a tradition from Ibn 'Umar. From *Muslim Devotions: A Study of Prayer Manuals in Common Use,* © Constance E. Padwick (1961) Used by permission of SPCK, London.

A *rahla* (Qur'an stand) worked in wood in Persia or West Turkestan, 1360. The work is signed Hasan, son of Suleiman of Ispahan. All rights reserved, The Metropolitan Museum of Art, Rogers Fund, 1910. (10.218)

Glossary

Allah	In Arabic, "God."
aya	"Sign" of God in the universe; "verse" of the Qur'an.
Ayatollah	Literally, "sign of God"; in Shi'ism in Iran, a religious leader who represents the Twelfth Imam.
dar al-Islam	The "Abode of Islam"; where Islam is believed and practiced.
dhimmi	"Protected citizens"; status for religious minorities in an Islamic society by which they are free to practice their religion and administer their community in return for loyalty and payment of a *jizya* (head tax).
fiqh	"Understanding" of the law; writings and schools of interpretation of the *shari'a*.
hadith	Authoritative collections of non-Qur'anic traditions of Muhammad's sayings and deeds.
Hajj	"Pilgrimage" to Mecca during pilgrimage month.
hanifs	Pre-Islamic pious believers in God, not belonging to a particular religion.
hijra	The "emigration" of Muhammad and his followers from Mecca to Medina for refuge in 622 A.D.; marks year 1 of Islamic calendar.
'Id al-Adha	The annual Feast of Sacrifice that ends the Hajj; commemorates Abraham's willingness to sacrifice his son, according to the Qur'an. (The hadith identify the son as Ishmael.)
'Id al-Fitr	Feast of Breaking the Ramadan Fast.
imam	"Leader" of communal prayers at the mosque.
Imam	In Shi'ism, a leader who is a special representative of the Prophet.
Injil	"Book of Jesus"; God's revelation to Christians.
Islam	"Submission" to God; total commitment to the authority and power of God; the faith, submission and practice of Muslim people.
jihad	"Struggle" or "effort" in the path of God; often used to describe a defensive "just war" to protect the interest of Islam; mistakenly called "holy war."
Ka'ba	Literally, "cube." A cube-shaped structure in Mecca, built around a sacred stone associated with Abraham.
khilafa	"Deputyship"; related to "caliph." Authority of community to govern itself under divine law.
masjid	Arabic word translated as "mosque"; see mosque.

mosque	Literally, "place of prostration"; the place or house of prayer.
Muslim	"One who is submitted to God"; one who recites and believes the *shahada*; a person whose religion is Islam.
qibla	The direction of Mecca, toward which Muslims face when praying.
Qur'an	"Recitation"; the book containing the messages from God recited by Muhammad and recorded by his followers.
rahma	Most important Arabic word for "mercy," a central attribute for God; root of divine names "The Merciful," "The Compassionate."
Ramadan	Month devoted to fasting from sunrise to sunset and to prayer.
riba	Interest; gain from loans of money or property; prohibited in Islam.
salam	"Peace"; a state of security, wholeness, well being involving all of life now and hereafter.
salat	Worship in the form of ritual prayer, five times daily.
shahada	"Bearing witness"; confession bearing witness to God's unity and Muhammad's messengerhood.
shari'a	"The way" or divine path of obedience to God; comprises the writings of the Qur'an and *hadith* as the guide for worship and ethical living.
Shi'a	"Partisans" or followers (of the Prophet's Household); Muslims who believe that leadership should come from descendants of Muhammad's family. One such Muslim is called, in English, a Shi'ite; the beliefs that characterize this part of the Muslim community are called Shi'ism.
shirk	"Association," the act of regarding anything as equal with God; idolatry.
shura	"Consultation"; the method of consensus by which the Muslim community governs itself.
Sufi	One who practices forms of Islamic mysticism.
sunna	"Way of acting"; the example of the Prophet.
Sunni	Popular name, derived from *sunna*, for the majority of Muslims.
sura	Chapter of the Qur'an, of which there are 114.
Torah	"Book of Moses"; God's revelation to the Jews.
umma	The whole community of Islam; the community God creates from whose who do Islam.
zakat	Contribution to charity required as a duty to God; about 2½ percent of one's wealth annually.

Acknowledgments

The editor and author are grateful to the following persons and publishers for permissions to print and reprint illustrations and excerpts.

Special thanks to *Aramco World*, published by Aramco, a corporation, and to its editor, Robert Arndt, for the use of photographs, illustrations and information both reprinted and adapted, from issues of the magazine as noted on pages 5, 7, 59, 61, 65, 72-73, 116-117, and for the cover photo.

Maps:
"The Islamic World", on page 3: adapted from *Islam: The Religious and Political Life of a World Community*, Marjorie Kelly, ed. (Praeger Publishers, a division of Greenwood Press, Inc., New York, 1984), p. 196. Copyright © 1984 by National Public Radio and the Foreign Policy Association. Used with permission.
"The Caliphate at Its Greatest Extent," on page 23. From R. M. Savory, editor, *Introduction to Islamic Civilisation* (Cambridge and New York: Cambridge University Press, © 1976), p. 17. By permission of the publisher. From pages 120-125 and 74 of the same volume, excerpts as noted on pages 6 and 54.
Table: on page 89. Table I, "Muslims and Christians in the World," reprinted from *Christians and Muslims Together: An Exploration by Presbyterians*, edited by Byron L. Haines and Frank L. Cooley. © 1987 The Geneva Press. Used by permission.

Two photographs from the manuscripts in the collection of the Pierpont Morgan Library, New York; reproduced by permission, as noted on pages 15 and 48.
Seven photographs from manuscripts and artifacts in the collections of The Metropolitan Museum, New York; reproduced by permission, as noted on pages 9, 10, 17, 27, 37, 92 and 135.
Three photographs courtesy of the United Nations, as noted on pages 34, 51 and 81.
A photograph on page 43 of the Ka'ba in Mecca, courtesy of the Information Office, Royal Embassy of Saudi Arabia, Washington, D.C.
Excerpts on pages 51, 67, 70 and 127 From: Yvonne Haddad, Byron Haines, Ellison Findly, eds., *The Islamic Impact* (Syracuse: Syracuse University Press, 1984), pages 75, 89-112, 114-118. By permission of the publisher.
Prayers on pages 28, 29, 41, 84 and 135 from: *Muslim Devotions: A Study of Prayer-Manuals in Common Use,* © Constance E. Padwick (1961). Reproduced by permission of S.P.C.K., London.
Excerpt on page 16 from: Nader Ardalan and Laleh Bakhtiar, *The Sense of Unity: The Sufi Tradition in Persian Architecture*, © 1973 by the University of Chicago. All rights reserved; used by permission of author and publisher.

Excerpt on page 20 from: Nawal El Saadawi, *The Hidden Face of Eve: Women in the Arab World.* Boston: Beacon Press, 1982, page 131. © 1980 by Nawal El Saadawi.

Information on page 39 about the Islamic calendar from: the Multifaith Calendar, with permission of the Multifaith Calendar Commitee of Canadian Ecumenical Action, Vancouver.

Sufi tale on page 71 from: *Mystical Dimensions in Islam*, by Annemarie Schimmel. © 1975, The University of North Carolina Press. Reprinted by permission.

Excerpt on page 76 from: "Ali: Still Magic," an interview by Peter Tauber in *The New York Times Magazine*, July 17, 1988. © 1988 by The New York Times Company. Reprinted by permission.

For the information, photograph and quotes on pages 106, 107, 109, 111, thanks to Sister Lucille Walsh and the participants in the Islamic-Christian Dialogue of the Archdiocese of Milwaukee and to *New Catholic World*, Nov.- Dec. 1988, for permission to reprint quotes.

For excerpts on pages 120-122, from: "The Muslim Experience in North America," by Yvonne Y. Haddad, in the Sept.-Oct. 1979 issue of "The Link," published by Americans for Middle East Understanding.

For information on page 125, thanks to the Interfaith Conference of Metropolitan Washington and its director, Clark Lobenstine, and for photographs on pages 212 and 125, to photographers Morton Broffman and Carl Hylton.

For information and excerpt on pages 130-131, thanks to the American Arab Ministry of the Presbytery of Detroit and the ministry's director, William Gepford.